A POLISH BOY
The Youngest Partisan

A POLISH BOY

The Youngest Partisan

A True Story

B F JOCHNOWITZ

First edition

Story Publications

ISBNs
979-8-9868422-0-2 {*Hardback*}
979-8-9868422-1-9 (*Paperback*)
979-8-9868422-2-6 (*Ebook—Kindle*)

TABLE OF
CONTENTS

PREFACE

THIS IS THE story of my husband's life. It is a subjective record of his own personal memories as close to accurate as I can make them from his tapes and personal accounts. For reasons of privacy, certain names in this book have been changed.

B F JOCHNOWITZ

INTRODUCTION

T HIS IS MY husband's true story. He had an excep-
tional memory and would often talk to me about
his childhood experiences during World War II. He
started to put them down on paper but found that his
pen wasn't fast enough so he decided to record them. We
would often discuss his thoughts and reactions during his
early life, and his wish to share his emotions as one of the
youngest survivors. I believe this book is timely and presents a fresh perspective of war and its casualties through
the eyes of an adventurous and heroic child. For this reason it is written in the first person. My hope is that those
who read it will understand this period in history and its
effect on a very young child.

PROLOGUE

I N THE VILLAGE of Zasov, Poland—not far from Krakow, in the house on a hill, a new baby boy squalls after the midwife's slap. She cleans him and gives him to his mother, Shanna, who holds him to her breast for feeding. Beads of perspiration appear on Shanna's forehead-strands of damp hair clinging to her face. She smiles and kisses her baby's keppy (dear little head). Her sister, Esther, is there and bends over to coo at the baby for a moment; then goes into the candy store in front of the house to tell the father, Vigdor, to come and meet his son.

Esther sees Vigdor pacing up and down. She notices how gray he is getting and how his once tall frame is starting to bend. When Esther approaches, he says, "Well?"

"You have a son. Come see."

Vigdor shrugs his shoulders and follows Esther into the bedroom. When he sees the child, there is no expression on his face. He bends over to kiss his wife and pats the baby's head. He says he has to leave and go to work to install a window. The mother looks disappointed for a moment but continues to cuddle her baby.

Esther runs across the road to get her husband, Yossef, and the rest of her family to come see the infant. The room is crowded, and the child's Aunt Esther, Uncle Yossef and the baby's cousins—Illya, Uri, Leah, and Basha—make a big fuss over him. Uncle Yossef, picks him up, holds him high and says a prayer of thanks that the baby and mother are healthy and for the child to grow strong. He returns him to his mother's arms.

Shanna says she wants to name her son Chiel after her father. He was a teacher, a writer and very smart. But best of all, he had a loving nature.

Eight days later, at the brit milah (rites representing God's covenant), Chiel's Uncle Yossef is named as his godfather.

For the first year of the boy's life, his mother is happy. Chiel is a beautiful child with light wavy hair, a sparkling smile, an infectious laugh, and a loving nature. The whole family adores him. But Vigdor is annoyed that his wife pays so much attention to him. When Chiel starts to walk, he gets into everything. This annoys his father who is impatient with him and keeps hollering, "No!" One day Chiel toddles over to the kitchen table and pulls down the tablecloth. He is so pleased with himself that he claps his hands. His mother starts to laugh, but it angers Vigdor, and he swoops the child up, spanks him hard, and throws him in his crib. When Shanna runs to pick her crying baby up, Vigdor says, "No, keep away-don't mix in." When he hears her say, "He's just a baby," he pushes her with such force that she falls.

Shanna and Vigdor were matched up by a friend of Uncle Yossef when Shanna was very young. He was a successful glazier and had a good business. When she first saw him, she was drawn to his good looks. They had interesting conversations and Shanna, who loved to read and write poetry, was impressed by his intelligence. They married and settled into a little house. She tended the candy store in front of the house, while he was at work. They were very happy the first months of their marriage, but when people didn't have enough money for his services or to buy candy, both businesses failed.

Times are getting worse. All the Jews in the village have very little money. Vigdor scrounges around to do whatever he can to earn some kind of living. He becomes more and more angry. Most of the time he takes out his anger on his son. His wife is afraid to interfere, so he beats the child until he screams so loud, Vigdor has to stop hitting him Shanna remains seated, with tears running down her face.

Uncle Yossef knows how "'crazy" Vigdor has become, and he and his family help Shanna and Chiel as much as they can. When Vigdor is not home they bring food and play with the little boy. Much of the time, they bring him back to their house. Uncle Yossef's hardware store is in the front of his house and there are always friends and neighbors there who are customers. They like to visit with Uncle Yossef and play with the little boy.

Uncle Yossef tells Chiel stories. He tells him he's a fine boy and is proud of him Aunt Esther feeds him and keeps kissing him. Chiel feels good when he is at his Uncle Yossef's house.

PART I

THE WAR YEARS

...the leaders of the Third Reich looked at the world in a way that made no sense to the rest of Western civilization; in particular, they believed that Jews were (literally) not human, and they were actually a pathogen that threatened (again, literally) to destroy all humanity and that therefore, by killing all Jews, the Third Reich was actually saving the entire human world from mortal danger. As far as the leaders of the Third Reich were concerned, killing Jews was one of the most important reasons for their states very being, and they devoted considerable resources scientific, economic, and human—to carrying it out.

The Holocaust: The Third Reich and the Jews, by David Engel—Copyright 2000—(Pearson Education Limited), Pg. 4.

CHAPTER 1:
VILLAGE OF ZASOV – JUNE 1939

IT'S DAWN. I wake up and need to pee. After putting on my shoes and coat, I start toward the door. My mother calls, "Where are you going, Chiel?"

"I need to pee."

"It's too cold outside, go in the pot." "I don't want to pee in the pot."

I run to the outhouse. I love to see the moon and the stars. It's winter and so cold I can see my breath and hear the snow crinkling under my feet.

While sitting I stare at the holes on the roof where icicles are hanging. Down in the deep hole frozen poop is covered with snow. I'm afraid I might fall in. Will the same thing happen to me?

The outhouse is better in the summer except for the smell and the flies. In the daytime through the cracks in the walls I see grass, wild flowers and our neighbor's horse in the field. At night, I listen to the crickets and try to count the stars.

We live in Zasov, Poland, and near our house on the hill is

the village square and all the buildings around it. I watch the kids go to school. Some of them are small like me, but most of them are bigger. They go through an iron gate into the schoolyard laughing and chasing each other. After a bell rings and they go inside the red brick building, I walk down to look at the colored pictures on the windows. When they're open, the kids scream at me, " *Zyd*", (kike). "Go home, kike. You can' t go here!" I don't understand. Why can't I go to school?

The church in the village has a big wooden door. The laughing kids go to that church. Maybe if I go there, I could go to school too. Sometimes, when no one is around, I walk up and put my hand on the door handle. But I'm afraid to go in because my Uncle told me not to.

Count Dubrovsky is the boss of the village. Sometimes I see him walking. He is very tall and has a funny mustache on his face. His house has a white wall around it. I ask uncle why horses, wagons and bicycles stand outside the wall. He says people go in and out all the time to ask for favors. Maybe I should ask the Count if he will let me go to school? I'll find out what Uncle thinks.

Uncle Yossef always reminds me that God created the universe and all its beauty, and He lets us live here on the earth.

"Is He everybody's boss?" I ask Uncle. "Yes."

"Then why doesn't He tell the kids at the school to stop calling me kike?" "He does, Chiel, but they don't listen."

When I'm not at my uncle's house, I sit outside and

play in the mud. I stay home more when Papa isn't there to beat me. Why is he always so mad?

My Aunt and Uncle say, "Stay close to our house because a criminal lives in the village. He's wanted for murder." Maybe I can ask that man to kill my father? I'm excited, but I better not tell my Uncle.

In the summer acorns fall off the trees, and little oak trees start to grow. I like to sit on the ground and plant my own oak trees. I put a blue mariner next to each of my acorns to guard them and I visit them every day to see how fast they're growing.

I don't have any friends my age, so I walk around the village by myself When I see a bigger boy coming toward me I say, "Do you want to play?"

He makes loud babbling scary sounds, "Ballaa, ballaa, ballaa," and starts to chase me. I go as fast as I can, but he's big and he catches me. I try to push him, "Go away!" He holds my arms and knocks me down. Then he sits beside me, sticks his tongue in my ear and touches my privates.

When I tell my mother and father about him, they just say, "Stay away from Crazy Manfred."

One day I'm pissing in the field next door. Pietrek, the big kid that lives there yells, "Get out of here, Jew. You don't belong here." Before I have a chance to finish, he comes over and puts a lit cigarette on my pisser. It makes a terrible sound and I scream. He laughs and twists the cigarette until he puts it out. It stops hurting in a few days, but it leaves a scar. I don't tell my parents, because they'll just say, "Stay away from him."

When it rains, the mud slides down my hill. I make mud balls and attach them to the end of a stick and am surprised at how far I can make them fly. I wish I could fly like that. I make believe I'm having a contest with a friend to see who throws them furthest.

In the winter I put snowballs on the end of a stick and throw them like they were mud balls. At first they fly like my mud balls but they don't go as far because they fall apart. I make snowmen and roll snowballs until they get very big. Sometimes I sled down the hill and sometimes I like to just roll myself down and giggle. It would be more fun if someone rolled down with me.

Gypsies drive by all the time. They steal chickens and all other kinds of stuff. One day they come by. A nice lady, wearing a bright shawl, says, "Come with me little boy." I say okay and sit next to her on the wagon. We start to go and a neighbor sees me and chases after us yelling, "My God they're stealing Chiel." The neighbor gets me, but I'm not happy. It would have been nice to be a Jewish Gypsy.

In Uncle's hardware store when I hear him and his customers talk about Germans and that Poland is in trouble, I ask Uncle what they mean. With a serious face he says, "There may be a war."

I'm scared. I'm not sure what "war" means. Uncle says, "We have to pray a lot." Somehow that makes me more frightened.

CHAPTER 2:
THE FAMILY – JULY 1939

M Y EYES ARE closed. Maybe if I can't see, the doctor won't stick the smelly glass on my back.

But I feel it again and scream "Stop, it hurts."

He says, "I know, Chiel, I'm almost done. You'll be better soon."

He dips another piece of cloth in a glass, lights a match to it, blows it out and sticks it on my back. I scream again.

When I get better and sit on the wooden floor in the kitchen, I set up my little blue mariners.

After stepping back a few feet, I bowl them over. Then set them up again. "Mama look what I can do!"

My mother, Shanna, is reading. She stops to watch me. "Very nice, tuteleh *(little man)."* She goes back to her book.

"Please tell me a story."

I love to hear about kings in beautiful palaces and make believe I'm there. But mostly Mama tells me stories about her sisters in America.

Papa's shop is in the next room, and when he has work to do, he's in a good mood. He's a glazier and measures large panes of glass on his worktable. He cuts and putties them into wooden frames. I like the smell of the putty and the sound of the blade when it cuts the glass. But most of the time he's grumpy, because he doesn't work much. He says, "It's hard to get work when you're a Jew."

"Why?"

"Don't ask so many questions."

There's not much food in the house. My father tries to earn extra money by buying some geese cheap. He makes them fatter, then sells them.

We sit on the old candy store floor in the front room of our house with a pan of water and a sack of corn. We take a handful of corn, roll it up, make a ball and shove it down the throats of the geese. They make a lot of noise and the smell is very bad. There are candy slivers left on the shelves of the store and the sweet smell of the candy mixed with the geese makes it a bit better. When I stuff the cornballs down the geese, they bite my finger. It hurts, so I pull my hand away. My father screams at me-over and over, "Feed the geese. Never mind your finger."

"No, I don't want to."

He's mad and moves to take off his belt. I shut my eyes tight and hope it doesn't land on me. But it does-over and over. I scream, "Stop Papa, I can't catch my breath." He doesn't stop.

I don't know why Papa hates me so much. My mother looks very sad, but she doesn't try to help because he beats her too.

I want to kill him, but I'm not big enough. I wait until dark, then bring one of my blue mariners to the outhouse. I wrap it up real good in a big leaf and throw it down the deep hole. Bending my head and rocking back and forth like when Uncle Yossef prays, I say, "Make my father go away."

My mother's sister and her family live down the road and when we're hungry we go to them. "You better not talk on me," warns my father.

I go to my aunt's a lot, even when I'm not hungry, because even though I'm little, my cousins play with me. Uri is 14 and has dark wavy hair. He's always combing it and smiling at himself in the mirror. "No wonder all the girls are crazy about me." Uri teases me about being so skinny, but sometimes he's nice and teaches me card games. The one I like the best is *Oko*. We use match sticks for money and bet. The best three cards win. Even when I get the numbers mixed up and I lose, Uri says I win.

Ilya is 20 and reads the newspaper. He's very strong and chops trees faster than anyone else.

He's not tall, but is extra wide. He gives me rides on his shoulders while he runs.

My auntie is always feeding me. She has twinkly eyes and squeezes me against her apron. "Darling, have something to eat. I want to fatten you up."

I love my Uncle Yossef best. He has a mustache and a beard and walks hunched over with his head down. He tilts his hat so that it almost covers his eyes and folds his hands behind his back. When I ask him a question, he pushes his hat to the back of his head, and says, "Hmm hmm hmm," before he answers me.

I like to go to Uncle's hardware store in the front of

his house. He lets me take a sour pickle from the barrel he keeps there. The customers are neighbors and sometimes pretend they are chasing me. I know they're just playing. But now they stay and talk to Uncle with serious faces. I don't understand some of their words-like *politics* and *Nazis.*

Uncle says he will teach me a prayer called *Modeh Ani* and I must say it every morning when I wake up.

"What's Modeh Ani?"

"A prayer to thank God for giving back your soul. He keeps it safe when you sleep.

What's a soul?"

"Hmmm ... hmm ... hmm. That's what you are inside. The thing that makes you special."

"Does He keep everybody's soul?"

"Yes."

"Where?"

"In heaven."

I am worried. "What if you get somebody else's soul?"

"That never happens."

"What if somebody dies? What happens to their soul?" "God gives it to a newborn baby."

In September 1939, Poland is invaded and soldiers march into Zasov. We see them everywhere. Uncle says they are Nazis and there will be some bad changes in our village. I wonder where these Nazis come from and why they are here.

CHAPTER 3

THE GHETTO –
NOVEMBER 1939

S INCE THE OCCUPATION of Poland, life is even harder than before. Jews are forced to wear yellow stars and can be picked up off the streets to work at manual labor. Nazis destroy synagogues and control everything a Jew can do.

When we hear rumors that the Germans are coming to take all the Jews away, my father looks at my mother and me. "I have to leave because they'll take all the men to ghettos and death camps. Don't worry, Women and children will be safe."

We know he's really running away and leaving us to die. My mother stares at the ground and says nothing. When he's gone, I look into her eyes and am so scared my stomach starts to growl.

We rush over to Uncle's house, my mother is crying. "Vigdor left us. He ran away and left us." Uncle says, "We're better off without him. We're going to stay together whatever happens."

My mother and her sister's family all hug. I'm glad that my father is gone. I feel safe with my uncle.

A few days later, the Germans go to every house in Zasov to take a census. All Jews will be taken away from the town. I stare out my window and see two German soldiers coming. They're wearing uniforms with shiny buttons and tall black boots.

When they reach my house, I'm afraid. One tall, blond soldier smiles and pats me on the head. He seems nice.

After they leave, my mother and I run down to the cellar and bury our silver candlesticks in the dirt floor. They're the most valuable things we own. She says when the war is over, we'll come back and find the candlesticks. Then we dress in many layers of clothes and take whatever food we have. There isn't much. Just a small bag of flour, some bread and a few cherries.

We go to stay at uncle's house so we will all be together when the Germans come to take us.

Auntie walks around the house, crying. Uncle and Ilya stuff two rucksacks with food, cooking supplies, fishhooks, string, medicines, and three cloth prayer bags. Uri adds shaving supplies, a mirror, combs, tobacco, a deck of cards and his metal cigarette roller. My mother stuffs the third rucksack with clothing.

Uncle tells us that he left money with his friend, Stashek, who owns a farm near the woods, that Stashek will supply us with food if he can smuggle it into the ghetto. Uncle puts the rest of his cash into a money belt.

"I don't want to go to a ghetto." Uri screams. "Germans and Poles are killing Jews in the forests. I want to run away and join a partisan group and kill them"

Uncle says, "No fighting partisan group will take us because we have women and a child. This is our best chance to survive. We need your help, Uri. We must stay together."

Uri calms down and agrees to come with us.

Ilya says nothing. He closes two of the rucksacks and hangs a shovel and an axe on each of them.

Uncle Yossef tells us to bow our heads, then he leads us in a prayer to protect us and to give us strength. When he lifts his head, I see tears in his eyes.

A few days later, the Nazis take all the Jews out of their houses and march us off to a ghetto.

My uncle, aunt, cousins, mother and I join the large group. I have to walk fast and run so I can keep up. My pants start to fall down. My mother holds one hand. I hold my pants up with the other.

Someone with a horse-drawn wagon calls to my mother and me to get on the wagon. On our way, the German soldiers on both sides of the road beat people who are too slow. They hit them over the head with rifle butts, knock them down. They kick and shoot many of them. I try to find the soldier who patted my head, but I don't see him.

I turn back to see my uncle and cousins walking. My Auntie Esther is holding on to Uncle Yossef so she can keep up. My cousins walk in front and behind her. The soldiers don't see how she struggles. The German soldiers yell, "Move faster." They hit or shoot anyone who complains.

I try not to move. Maybe if we are very still, they won't notice us. I don't want them to hit or shoot Mama.

I sit on the wagon and hold the bread, flour and cherries. The ride knocked some cherries into the flour. I look down and keep myself busy by taking the cherries out of the flour, wiping them off and eating them one by one. I don't want to watch the mean Germans.

The ride is bumpy. I feel like throwing up, but I don't. My mother sits with her eyes closed. She's crying. I reach over and pat her back. She grabs my hand and kisses it. I turn and wave at my uncle, but he doesn't see me. He's helping my aunt and staring at the soldiers. I know he prays they don't hurt my aunt.

Then I see the ghetto up ahead, with stone walls all around it. All the windows and doors to the rest of the city are bricked up. We go through an entrance that traffic can pass through. I glance back searching for my uncle's family. Did they make it this far? We are put into an apartment with three other Jewish families. The guards say we are lucky, because some of the Jews have to live on the street. My cousins are with us. I ask where my aunt and uncle are. Ilya says their mother was tired and had to drop back. Uncle Yossef stayed with her.

We try to settle into the crowded apartment. I don't like it because it is very noisy. I trip over someone's bag. There are so many people here I'm afraid someone will step on me, but Mama helps me up. As we decide where our family will sleep and eat, we are happy when Uncle Yossef arrives. But he is crying.

Uncle heard the Germans were going to shoot all the older women. They promised they wouldn't shoot my aunt if Yossef gave them money.

"I gave them all the money I had, but they shot her anyway."

We cried until we had no more tears. I think how good Auntie Esther was to me. How she always made sure I was warm enough and had enough to eat. I will miss her so very much.

Uncle Yossef leads us in the Kaddish (prayer for the

dead) in memory of Auntie Esther. We are very quiet, because uncle doesn't want any of the guards to hear. He is afraid they'd kill us for practicing our religion. Afterwards we all join hands and Uncle says another soft prayer to get us through these hard times.

I ask if I can go outside. My mother says I can if I stay close to the house. I walk toward a crowd on the street and see people selling their things in the market square. A German policeman checks the papers of some Jews. I go a little further and see German soldiers forcing men to dig ditches in an empty lot. I wonder why they're doing this. I see other soldiers watching the Jews finishing up the wall around the ghetto.

I am sad and miss the little hill where I played with mud balls. I miss my uncle's house. It would have been good to be there again without my father. Why are we here?

I turn to go back to our apartment, but I don't know where I am I'm lost. I walk around for a while and smell something wonderful. Like the sherbet my uncle used to buy me. It would be nice if I could have some now. I follow the smell to a cellar that used to be a store. I see mostly empty shelves and some melting things in a case.

The man there says, "Can I help you?" "No, I don't have any money."

"Do you like sherbet?"

I nod my head and he scoops some in a cone. "Here you are, young man. Eat it quickly before it melts."

I lick it very fast and I'm happy with the delicious taste in my mouth.

When I finally find my way home, my mother yells at me for wandering away. She makes me promise I won't do that again. When I tell her about the sherbet, she smiles and hugs me very hard. I ask her why we had to come here. She says all the Jews in Poland had to leave their homes and go to ghettos. A new law the Germans made. She says we might have to go somewhere else before we can go home. I ask her when we can go home. She sighs and says, "When the war is over."

I don't understand.

After a few weeks, we are piled into trucks and taken to a work camp. My mother was right.

CHAPTER 4

THE CAMP– DECEMBER 1939

M Y MOTHER, UNCLE Yossef, Basha, Uri, Ilya and I sit together on one of the trucks, but Leah is forced off. She kisses Uncle and tries to hug the rest of the family, but the soldiers drag her away and push her on a different truck.

"Mama, why can't she come with us?"

"I don't know. Maybe there isn't enough room for her."

"But why, she could have kept me on her lap. Will we see her there?"

"I don't know Chiel. Try to be quiet my love."

When we arrive at the camp, my uncle asks where my Cousin Leah's truck is. They say it went to a bigger camp. When he asks why, the soldiers don't answer and push us all into the barracks. Men's cots are on one side of the room, women's on the other. My mother and I share one cot and Basha is on the next one. My uncle, Uri and Ilya are on the other side of the room.

Every day, the guards shout at all the grown-ups to go outside. Both men and women work on the edge of the camp grounds. The camp hasn't been open long and the prisoners are to finish building it. The little kids stay in the barracks most of the time.

The workers take logs off a tremendous pile and chop up the wood. It's winter and bitter cold. They rub their hands to try to keep them warm. There are barrels with fire in them and some workers warm their hands over the barrels. Sometimes the little kids bring them water in cups from the barracks. When I pass out the cups of water, I see an axe. I take it and try to chop some wood too, but my uncle grabs it away from me.

I watch the trains going by. Day after day I hear the slow clickety-clack of cattle cars. The shrieks and the faces I see in the small barred windows scare me. I run back and hide in the barracks.

There are barbed-wire fences around the camp. Uncle says they're electrified. The wire extends beyond the top of the fence.

I ask Uncle, "Why are those people hanging on the lines?"

"They tried to escape by climbing over the fence but didn't make it. They are dead."

It's windy and the bodies are waving in the wind. They remind me of charcoal cut-out dolls.

They have clothes on but all I can see are black figures.

I wonder if electrified is a kind of gun. I better stay away from that fence.

When it's not so cold, I wish I could stay outside with kids from the other barracks and play. I hear machine guns, and I'm afraid. I stay out of the way until it's time to go with my family and stand with all the others in a long line to get our one meal. They give us stale bread and some brown stuff. I eat the brown stuff and save half of my bread.

After we eat, the adults go back to work until dark.

Some of them are shot because they're too weak to work. I hear the shots as I run to the barracks. I hide the bread under my blanket.

At night, when my mother returns, I say, "Mama, I saved some bread for you." "No, my love. I'm not hungry. You eat it."

I'm always hungry, so I eat the bread.

One day, the guards come to get Basha. They don't say why. When she doesn't return, my uncle asks the guard where she is. He tells Uncle that they found out Basha was a Zionist and a member of an underground movement, so they shot her. My uncle says that isn't true. The guard just shrugs.

My cousin, only 15 years old, is buried in a mass grave outside the camp. Again we say the Kaddish in memory of another member of our family. We whisper it fast and try to be quiet. We don't want the guard to catch us. My mother hugs me. We cry all night.

Between sobs, I wonder if they're killing our family one by one. Will I be next?

I've been in the camp for a few months. My cousin, Ilya, comes to me while I'm giving out the water. Making sure the guard doesn't see him with me, he tells me that two guards said that tonight they will shoot all the children under 14 and all the men over 40. Ilya says we'll escape, but first I must go to the barracks and hide under my bunk.

"When the guard walks by, I don't want you to breathe."

He sounds angry, "Don't come out from under the bunk until we get you or you'll die."

I run back to the barracks and do what Ilya told me. I get under the bunk and stay. I stop breathing when a soldier comes in to check. I can see his shiny boots from my hiding place. They remind me of the German's who came to our house and patted me on the head. But this German isn't nice. He wants to kill kids. I hold my breath until he goes away. Then I hear the machine guns. And I know all the other children are dead.

At the end of the work day, my cousin sneaks into my barracks. He leads me out, saying we are going to escape. We go to a spot at the barbed wire fence. One by one, my other cousin, uncle and mother join us. It is almost dark. From the tower, guards watch with machine guns and shine a search light all around the camp. There are two guards walking around the camp with guns. When the light and the guards are in a different area, we manage to dig a hole under the wire using sticks to loosen the earth. Then each of us, carefully squirms under the barbed wire and crawls into the field toward the forest. When the search light is above us, we freeze and lie flat.

When we are out of the search light's reach, we stand up and run. My uncle stops. Crying, he points to the mass grave where Basha is buried. He says a silent prayer, then we continue to run toward the forest.

CHAPTER 5:

THE FOREST –
JANUARY 1940

THERE'S A FULL moon, but it is hidden by the clouds most of the time. Uri and Ilya walk ahead of us. My mother is behind them and my uncle and I follow. We're moving fast through some fields. Sometimes when I look up I can see the moon. It seems to be chasing us. After a while, we have a hazy view of the woods. As we go through some tall grass, we can't see anything.

Our worn shoes and clothes get muddy. My uncle is wheezing. My mother is limping, because her shoes have holes on the bottoms. I can't walk anymore, so Ilya hoists me up on his shoulders.

We finally reach the forest and keep walking all night only stopping to rest. We stay close together because it's very dark and we're afraid we'll be separated. The branches scratch our faces and hands. It's late morning when we arrive in a very dense part of the woods.

Uncle Yossef says, "This is it. This will be our first camp. Let's rest a while, then we'll dig an underground shelter and a latrine."

We cup our hands and drink from a nearby stream. Then we wash our faces and hands. Uri stops to pull a comb out of his pocket.

Uncle Yossef says, "Uri, what are you doing? There are no girls here. Get serious."

Then he reminds us that we have to make our camp look as if no one lives here. "Don't light a fire during the daytime because people can see the smoke for miles. We'll have a campfire at night, but don't cut down any trees. Use only fallen branches. Put out the fire before dawn. Throw the cold ashes down the latrine."

Ilya and Uri dig a shelter inside a small hill under some fir trees. We have enough space to sit up inside and we practice getting in and out of the narrow opening. They dig a deep hole for the latrine far away from the shelter.

Uncle tells us to throw some earth in after we use the latrine and cover it with branches. "Don't wander too far. If you hear someone coming, scatter and hide. Then when they're gone, run for the shelter. The last person to crawl must hide the entrance."

Uncle Yossef carries a precious tin of matches in his pocket. He makes sure they always stay dry. We find some branches and make a campfire on the first night. Uncle and his two sons huddle near the fire and fall asleep. My mother holds me close and sings to me. I'm happy because she's taking care of me and my father isn't here to beat us

Before I fall asleep, I see shapes in the flames that lick the night air. I listen for the loudest crackle from the fire and the night sounds of the forest. I check to see how high the sparks will fly before they go out.

The next morning, I wake up to a dead fire. Uncle Yossef, Uri and Ilya are standing under some trees and praying. When they're done, we throw the cold campfire ashes down the latrine and cover it with branches. We scatter leaves to hide the campfire site. Then we look for breakfast. The dandelion greens we pick are kind of bitter, but we eat them anyway. Mostly we find patches of grass. We sit down and eat our grass and dandelion breakfast. Ilya and Uri talk about the places where they worked and the girls they knew. My mother pretends not to listen.

We get diarrhea and take turns running to the latrine. I squat and can barely straddle the hole. I'm afraid of falling in. I have to use leaves to wipe. Uri says that he doesn't feel clean, so he goes to the stream and puts his bottom in the cold water. Ilya and I do the same. Uncle Yossef sees the three of us in the water and asks us what we're doing. We turn around, bend over and wiggle our bare behinds. Uncle laughs.

He says, "Come with me, Chiel, it's time for your lesson."

I dry myself the best I can and go with him to sit under a tree. He clears the ground off, picks up a stick then starts to write some Hebrew letters in the dirt." I ask him, "Are people trying to kill us because we're Jewish?"

"You ask very hard questions, Chiel. Yes, a lot of people hate us because we're Jewish. Until the war is over we are not free to do whatever we want."

"But why?"

"Because the Germans think they are better than we are. They want to kill us all. But there are a lot of good people in the world who see that this is wrong. After the war is over, no one will chase us. We'll be able to stop running and to be free and happy."

I pick a stick up and try to copy some of the letters. "Is

that why the kids call me kike when I am near their school and say I can't go there?"

"Yes, they don't know any better."

"Well, I thought if I went to church like the other boys, maybe they would let me go to their school."

"No Chiel, we don't worship in a church. We pray in a synagogue and we're proud of our religion just as they're proud of theirs."

"Do they hunt Jews in America too?"

"No."

"Maybe you can go to America and take us with you."

"We'll try and get there after the war, Chiel."

Uncle Yossef is tired of my questions and tells me to go and talk to my cousins.

We need to get food. Uncle Yossef makes plans to go to Stashek Kuczinski 's farm. Stashek is uncle's friend who said he'd help us if we needed it.

We get up before dawn. The men say their prayers. Uncle Yossef talks to his sons about the kinds of supplies we need and about the timing of the trip. Ilya says, If we leave here this afternoon, we can get to Stashek's farm late at night when his children are asleep and get back to the forest while it's still dark.

I ask my cousins if I can go with them. They say I'm too young. We sit and talk until it's time to leave. Uri jokes around and tells us, "It'll be tomorrow morning before you know it, and we'll be back with lots of food."

We hug them and Uncle says, "Be careful and come back to us safe."

After they leave, Uncle reads his Bible, and my mother is reciting something to herself I sit next to her and ask what she is saying. "It's a poem that I memorized."

"What's a poem?"

"A beautiful way of describing things."

I tell her I want to hear more about America and her two sisters who live there

I pick a leaf off the ground and start to tear it to keep my fingers busy. My mother says, "They wrote to me about New York and the Empire State building. It's the tallest building in the world and has elevators that *worn* you up to the top in a few minutes."

I tear another leaf. "What's an elevator?"

"You stand in a box that lifts you up or down so you don't have to use the stairs. New York also has the Statue of Liberty, a giant lady with a torch who shines her welcoming light and offers freedom for refugees from all over the world, like she's going to do for us some day."

We miss Uri and Ilya. I don't feel like eating our grass and mushroom supper. When it starts to get dark, we gather some firewood. Uri usually starts the fire, but Uncle Yossef tells me I am old enough to do it now. First, I build the fire slowly with pine needles and small dry branches, then uncle lights it and when there's a strong flame, I add the wood

Ilya and Uri walked for many miles to Stashek's farm. It stood at the edge of the woods and my cousins had to be very careful not to be seen. They didn't want to get caught and they didn't want Stashek to get in trouble. He risked his life and his family's life to help us survive. He provided as much food and supplies as my cousins could carry and also gave them a sword to give to Uncle to use as a weapon or a tool. My cousins made it back to our campsite before dawn.

After they return, they are exhausted but happy we have food to keep us going. Uncle Yossef tells us we must make the food last. We will have two small meals a day. If we're still hungry, we'll pick berries, nuts and mushrooms.

We store this new food supply in the shelter and are in a good mood. This is more food than we've had in months. My cousins are my heroes.

CHAPTER 6:
PARTISANS

THE FOOD LASTS for a couple of weeks. During the rest of the winter, we steal food from farms at the edge of the forest. Not when it snows, because it's too hard to run with no shoes and rags on our feet.

As soon as the snow stops, we see the ground. It's time to move again. We wait for a moonless night and raid the closest farm. After filling our sacks from the heaped potatoes, we take rags off scarecrows to help keep us warm. When there are clothes drying on a line, we grab them too. Before dawn, we return to our shelter looking like the scarecrows we steal from.

Cousin Uri's specialty is to go into the hen house and scoop up a couple of chickens, wring their necks and throw them in a sack. He's so fast they don't make a sound.

One night, Uri tries to steal a live calf He puts a rope around it and pulls while we're running away. The calf is pretty strong and he has a tug of war with Uri. The dogs hear us, bark and wake up the farmers. Even when they come out with shotguns and start to shoot, Uncle Yossef and Ilya can't stop laughing at Uri who is tugging the calf until he finally lets go and the calf wins.

I always run last. Ilya falls back to get me. He carries

me on his shoulders while Uri screams, "Leave the little bastard. He'll get us all killed."

At the campfire, we cook the chickens and the potatoes. I'm responsible for doling out the food. I get even with Uri by giving him the smallest portion. When I make a face at him he tries to slap me, but my uncle won't let him.

One day, we're gathering dry branches for the fire and searching for whatever might be safe to eat. My cousins tease me and say my pile of branches is less than theirs.

We hear rustling of the leaves and we scatter and hide. A group of people are coming toward us. Not Nazis. They have no guns and are dressed in rags. When Uncle Yossef and my mother go to meet them, we follow. The men tell us they're partisans and have been hiding in the woods since the war started. A group of fifteen people including one woman and her young son. They're happy to see us and tell us there are many different partisan groups in the forest. Some of them formed communities, but they didn't want children or women. They offer to join us. Together, we would total 20. Smaller than the other partisan communities.

After talking for a while, my uncle and Avram agree to camp together as long as each group finds food. Avram tells us to be extra careful after the winter is over, because it will be easier for the Germans and Polish collaborators to find us. We must be ready to run at a moment's notice. Uncle Yossef agrees and says we're always ready. If necessary, we can create a shelter somewhere else.

I'm the lookout in the forest and sit away from the campsite for hours by myself and listen. I have very good hearing and eyesight. While I sit and watch, I talk to myself and to the deer and eat grass with them. I also talk to God about the sky and shooting stars and about being a Jew. Why didn't the kids let me go to kindergarten? I loved to see the colored cutouts on the school windows. Why did they call me "kike?" Why is it worse to be a Jew than a deer?

The winters are unbearable. Only frozen potatoes are stored in the shelter. When we have no other food, we eat the frozen potatoes and talk about freedom. We have constant bouts of diarrhea and are infested with lice. When uncle and I sit together and the lice bother us, we play a game competing to see who can kill more of them. We do anything to pass the time and get our minds off the itching.

I make friends with Samuel, the twelve-year-old-boy. Even though I'm only five-and-a-half, Samuel shows me how to roll leaves and smoke them. He teaches me how to wrestle. He will be bar mitzvahed next year when he is thirteen. I never had a friend before. Sometimes we sit together and are very quiet watching for the hunters. We know we always can talk around the campfire later.

I'm by myself, leaning against a tree trunk at the lookout spot. To keep from being hungry, I try to find something to eat. While I chew on clover and listen to the birds chirp, I watch them fly off. Where are they going? It's nice they're free and can go wherever they want. I'm thinking about all the times I sat on the hill near my house in Zasov. The trees and the grass are nicer in the forest.

I hear a strange sound. My ears perk up. Is it a bird or

the hunters? Just as I start to run and warn the others, someone comes out of the bushes and tackles me to the ground.

"Surprise!" It's Samuel.

After my heart stops beating loud, I try to wrestle and beat him up for scaring me. He's much bigger than I am, but he lets me win.

At night we get silly. When Uncle Yossef talks, we don't listen and make faces at each other. We start to laugh for no reason at all. Unusual for me. But Uncle understands I'm just being a kid and when he yells at me, he doesn't mean it. He tells the rest, "It doesn't hurt anything. Let the boys laugh. God knows there isn't enough laughter these days."

The Poles know there are Jews hiding in the forest. They hunt for us every couple of weeks. The dense wooded areas have so much underbrush it's very hard to walk. Because we are so well camouflaged, the forest is our friend. But, when they do find us, someone always gets shot.

One day, Samuel and I are at the look-out spot, not talking. We hear a stirring of the underbrush in the distance. We run as fast as we can to warn the others. The other partisans drop what they're doing, scatter and hide.

I'm running with Samuel. When I turn to tell my friend to go to our favorite hiding place, I see him on the ground.

He isn't moving. There's blood around his head. I can't stop or I'll get shot too. Tears stream down my face. All I can think of is my friend won't be able to have his bar mitzvah.

When Samuel's mother, Tanya, is told about her son,

she cries and can't stop. She screams she wants to die too. But Avram comforts her and tells her that she has to go on for Samuel.

We move on to make another camp. I can't stop thinking and have trouble sleeping. My mother tries to comfort me. I keep asking, "Why Samuel? Why wasn't it me too?"

"We don't know." My mother says. "Maybe God wants you to keep helping us to stay safe by being a lookout and warning us when trouble is coming. You must keep doing that for us and for Samuel's family."

One night at the campfire, I overhear my uncle talking. Uncle Yossef tells my mother and cousins it's time that I know what happened to my father. I'm afraid and I interrupt, "What about my father? He's not here is he?"

Uncle says, "No. He's dead."

"Dead? What happened?" I remember the prayers I said when my father slammed me with his big calloused hands. Could it be God answered me?

Uncle says, "While he was running away, the German soldiers caught him. They beat him, then the dogs did a job on him."

I hated my father, but when I hear this, I start to scream. "It's my fault! I wanted him to die, but I didn't want dogs to kill him."

My mother says, "It's not your fault. They killed everyone who tried to run away."

I can't be consoled and cry most of the night. When I finally do fall asleep, I have a nightmare.

German shepherds try to devour me. I see my father's dying face.

I develop a terrible stutter.

CHAPTER 7:
ALWAYS RUNNING

I T'S 1941 AND winter again. We've been in the forest for a year. There is never enough food in winter. We're starving and freezing. Even with so many deer, they're too big to kill. We're being hunted and need to remember that the Nazis or Poles are never far away. We must prepare ourselves to run at any moment, like the deer we see in the forest.

Most of the time, our discussions around the fire at night are: When will we stop being hungry? When will we be free? When will the war be over? How much longer will this go on? Maybe we should surrender-it would be much easier. Let's give up.

Uncle says, "No. We owe it to our dead loved ones to survive. We will never give up."

Uncle Yossef has a sore on his fingertip and it becomes infected. He tries to keep it clean but after a week it gets worse and turns black. After calling the group together, he puts his gangrene fingertip on a tree stump. With one swipe of his sword, he cuts it off. I blink my eyes. Did I really see this?

Then he says, "We must do whatever we can to stay alive. We'll be free by Passover next spring. Just hang on."

Passover comes and goes.

We *must* survive until Rosh Hashanah, or Chanukah

or whatever holiday is next. Whenever a bad thing happens to us, uncle promises we will be free when the next holiday arrives. He gives us the strength to keep going. One holiday at a time.

Our only way to keep track of time is the change of the seasons. When it's spring and summer, life is better. We live on wild blueberries, strawberries, nuts and different kinds of grass. We find mushrooms and wild crab apples and suffer with diarrhea most of the time. Although we can gather food and are not so cold, our enemies stalk us more often. There's no snow to hinder them.

Even though we're in constant danger, Uncle often reminds us it would be worse in a concentration camp. In the forest we're free to roam. We have some control over our lives and are not captives.

My Uncle Yossef knows the right mushrooms to pick and eat and which ones are poisonous. He teaches me about nature, the universe and religion. Nobody else wants to talk to me except my mother. I'm a little kid and a pain in the *tush*.

After the death of Samuel, my mother often stays at the lookout with me during the day. She knows how much I miss my friend and holds my hand while we sit listening. At night by the fire, she tells me stories. She used to read and knows many things about America from books and from her sisters' letters.

"Are your sisters happy in America?" "Yes. It's a wonderful country."

"Why did they go to America, while the rest of the family stayed in Poland?"

"Well, their husbands knew America was a free country and they made enough money to buy tickets to go."

"What's a free country?"

"A free country is one that allows everybody to be treated the same and they can believe in God however they want to. The Jews have the same chances as everyone else if they work hard."

"Why isn't Poland a free country?"

Mama pulls me over and I put my head on her lap. She takes a deep breath. "It wasn't always that way. Many years ago when the Jews were treated unfairly and were thrown out of other countries, they looked for a place to be safe. They found it in Poland. It was a poor country then, but the Jews helped make it a nice place to live. Over time, many Jews came to Poland. They had talents in crafts and commerce and manufacturing goods. There were many Jewish writers and musicians and they were even soldiers in the Polish Army."

"Why did it change?"

"The good years for the Jews in Poland started to come to an end when it was divided up between Russia and Germany. Antisemitism—that means people who hate the Jews-from Germany and Russia as well as all of Europe-was growing. Soon most of the Polish Jews were poor because of the overall bad economy and by anti-Jewish laws that the government passed. Jews, like us, were kept separate from everyone and we couldn't defend ourselves against the bad things that happened to us."

"Do you miss your sisters?" "Oh, I do."

"Tell me about them."

Mama thinks a moment. "We all look alike and they're good cooks. When we go to America they'll make delicious meals for us."

"Auntie Esther used to make me meals. She was nice to me."

We talk about our life in Zasov, but we never talk about when my Father hit me.

How I miss playing outside with mud balls and running over to Uncle Yossef's store where I reached into his pickle barrel and crunched on a crisp sour pickle. How I used to sit on the hill and watch people in the village.

"Mama, remember when I played with my mariner set all the time. I loved that set."

"I remember, sweetheart."

"Maybe we should have buried it in the cellar next to the silver candlesticks."

I see a little smile. But she doesn't answer.

I talk about the time a gypsy tried to steal me and how I wished I could have become a Jewish gypsy. "Where are the gypsies now?"

"The Nazis don't treat the gypsies any better than the Jews. Many of them ended up in concentration camps."

That makes me sad.

One day, while my mother is sorting rags at the camp, I hear something at the lookout spot. I know the hunters are here and I run to the campsite to warn everyone. I grab my mother's hand. We need to run. To hide. We hear the hunters behind us and run very fast through the woods.

Then my mother can't catch her breath and stops. "Come Mama. Come. They're catching up."

Her eyes are sad and she drops the rags. "You go, Chiel. I can't run any more, but you must go."

I wish I were bigger so I could pick her up, like Ilya

picks me up. But I am six years old and can only say, "But Mama they have guns." "Chiel, go now!"

I don't know what else to do, so I run away.

After the hunters are gone, the partisans reunite at the campsite and prepare to move again. My mother isn't here. I tell Uncle what happened. He says I did the right thing to keep running. That I am brave. But I don't agree. I should have stayed with my mother.

My stutter is even worse. I have trouble getting a sentence out of my mouth. I don't want to speak ever. I cry all the time.

Tanya, Samuel's mother, sits with me at the campfire and says she knows how I feel. She misses Samuel a lot too. But it helps her to know he's watching over her. She says my mother is watching over me and will always be in my heart. Tanya's words help a little, but I still feel awful. Her voice is nice. She sings me to sleep at night. I think she wishes I were Samuel.

I never wish she were my mother.

CHAPTER 8:

SPRING IN THE FOREST

U NCLE YOSSEF AND my cousins take turns sitting
with me at the lookout site. I miss my mother. I feel
a little better when I'm with them, but most of the time
I'm alone with nobody to talk to. I think about God at
night and stare up at the heaven and see shooting stars. Is
God throwing them from the sky? I run into the woods
to catch them. I know He made the sky and those beautiful stars. If this is true and God made the heaven and the
world, why did he let my mother die?

My cousin, Uri, tries to improve my mood by
wrestling me to the ground and tickling me. I laugh hard
and he says, "See you can still laugh."

One day Uri says, "Come here, I want to talk to you."
I think he's being nice. After I sit next to him, I get itchy
and feel things crawling all over me. When I see a mound
of red ants, I scream and jump around trying to get rid
of them. Uri keeps pointing at me and laughing. "What's
wrong with you? Can't you take a joke?"

At night while I pass out the food, I get back at him
and give him the smallest burnt potato I can find. When
he complains, I say "What's wrong Uri? Can't you take a

joke?" I start to run away. When he can't catch me, Uncle Yossef and Cousin Ilya look on and think it's funny.

The next day, Uri and I are trying to find mushrooms and grass to eat. We find some nice clover. He says, "Open your mouth, I think you have clover in your teeth." When I do, he stuffs a handful of dandelion puffy seed-balls into my mouth.

They make me gag. "Okay Uri. Wait until tonight. I'll get you for this."

Soon, I get back to normal. But my mother is always on my mind. I think I see her everywhere and I remember our talks. Now she will never see America or taste her sisters' cooking.

There are only 18 people left in our group. During the warm weather Uncle Yossef leads us in prayer every Friday night-or the one night a week he guesses is Friday. He says it's good to try to be as normal as possible. After saying a few Sabbath prayers, we have a little extra morsel of food for the Kiddish and sing one of the songs we remember. Uncle Yossef says we must keep up our faith and traditions. Afterwards, we feel better.

We make many runs to farms and gather clothes and food for the coming winter. Our new campsite is near a stream. After washing ourselves and splashing around in the water, it feels good to be clean. Soon it will freeze over and we won't be able to wash.

Uncle Yossef uses his sword to cut our hair and get rid of the lice. He almost scares me to death when he teases us by waving it around before he grabs hunks of our hair and cuts it. My Uncle Yossef can do anything.

But I miss my mother. Now I won't have a father or a mother for the rest of my life.

CHAPTER 9:
HIDDEN CHILD

THE WINTER OF 1943 is the worst. The mounds of snow are too high for us to raid nearby farms for food. We've been starving for days and the snow keeps falling. We grab handfuls and eat it just so we have something in our belly.

Ilya and Uri create a snow shelter for each of us. I crawl in mine through the small entrance. My body creates some warmth, and I'm protected here from the falling snow. I feel sleepy and imagine Auntie Esther giving me some hot soup and urging me to eat. I picture my Uncle's house and the pickle barrel. I lose track of time. When the snow stops, my uncle calls for me to crawl out and my eyes squint getting used to the light

My uncle and cousins sit around me. Uncle says, "Chiel, I love you, and will always protect you. You are only eight years old and don't have enough fat on your body for a boy your age to survive in this weather. Ilya will take you to my Polish friend, Yaskovich. Remember him? You saw him at my store in Zasov."

"Yes. He used to talk to me."

"I trust him. He'll help you. He has four children, and Ilya will ask him to pretend you are a member of his family."

Ilya gives me more rags to put on for added warmth

and takes my hand. We start walking. After a short time, my feet are getting numb, and I keep falling down. Ilya, scoops me up and puts me on his shoulders.

He starts to sing. I like his voice. He tells me to sing too. I don't have a very good voice. When he hears me, he laughs and says, "Chiel, when you grow up, you better study to become a professor or a lawyer. You'll never earn a living by singing."

When he keeps talking to me, I forget where we are going. Soon we see the end of the woods and he stops and puts me down. He says, "Become familiar with where you are now and how we are going to get to Yaskovich's farm."

He points to a nearby tree, then breaks a couple of branches on both sides. He pulls some bark off the tree and uses the pointed edge of the branch to mark an X. "Remember this place. You'll be safe at Yaskovich's house, but if for any reason you must leave, run to this spot and stay here. One of us will try to check this tree every day. Do you understand?"

"Yes. Are you sure you'll be able to find me?"

"Don't worry. That's just in case of an emergency. You'll probably stay at the Yaskovich's house until we are able to get some food. Then we'll come and get you."

Ilya knocks on the farmer's back door. He tells him how much we are suffering and asks him to save my life. Yaskovich hesitates for a moment. He calls to his wife and they talk it over. Then his wife hugs me. It feels good like when my mother used to put her arms around me. I miss her so much.

They welcome me into their home and give Ilya food to bring back. I almost cry when he leaves, but I don't.

When the kids ask me to play with them, I feel better.

They are told to pretend I am one of their brothers and that's the way they treat me. This is the first time I ever played with kids my own age. I don't talk to them very much because I stutter, but we have fun anyway. Soon, we are at the supper table and I see all the food. They urge me to eat, but I can't. I keep thinking of my uncle and cousins starving. The boy close to my age, Gerek, says, "If you don't eat, we won't be able to play." The food is good, but I'm not used to eating very much and soon I'm too full. I can't eat any more.

After supper, all the kids are told to take a bath. Gerek shows me where to bathe and wash my hair. He hands me some of his clothes. After I'm clean I put them on, but they are way too big and the pants fall on the floor. He gives me a belt so they will stay up.

They teach me a new game. All of the kids are sitting in a circle. When I see they have the same color hair and eyes as I do, I feel safer. I look as if I could be their real brother.

I start to feel very tired and yawn. It's time for bed and Gerek's mother says he will have to sleep with me. He doesn't mind and gives me a pair of his pajamas. The bed we sleep on has clean sheets, a pillow and a warm blanket like I used to have before the war. I don't have any trouble falling asleep.

Before I know it, Gerek is waking me up for breakfast and morning chores. I learn to milk the cow and do the other jobs all the kids do. The family is very nice. They're taking a big chance by hiding me. They are not at all like the Polish people who hunt and try to kill us.

One day when we're sitting in the living room, there is a strong knock at the door. Yaskovich grabs me by the hand and leads me to a hiding place in the kitchen. I squeeze into a narrow space behind the chimney.

He goes back and opens the door. I hear a German soldier asking if he is hiding any Jews. The farmer says, "No."

I don't think the soldier believes him. The questions continue.

I am terrified that the farmer will give me up. I soil my pants. My stomach is burning and my feet are paralyzed. It would be easier to stay and die than to run again. My feet finally move. I tiptoe to the back door, unlatch it and run toward the forest.

I run so fast my heart is thumping. After a long time, I turn to see if anyone is chasing me. I don't see anyone, so I keep on running. It doesn't take very long for me to get to the spot Ilya marked. It's getting dark. I have a hard time finding the X, but I see a tree and a light spot where some bark is scraped. I take a closer look and find the X.

A feeling of relief comes over me. Now all I have to do is wait and watch out for strangers or unfriendly animals. I climb up the tree, sit on the closest strong branch and lean up against the trunk. My eyes are closed and I hear the night sounds of the forest. It's a cold, clear night and the stars are bright. I see the formations of stars my uncle and I used to try and name. There are some shooting stars but tonight I'm too tired to chase them. I wonder when Ilya will come. I doze off and the rustling of leaves and underbrush wake me. Am I in danger? I'm afraid. My heart starts to jump again until I see my cousin. I whisper his name. He looks up and when he sees me he pulls me down.

He has his knapsack with him so we can steal some food on the way back to the woods. He puts me on his shoulders, and we stop at a small farm to grab some potatoes. On the way to our camp, I tell him about the little kids at the Yaskovich house and how much fun I had. I ask, "Ilya why are some Polish people so nice and others want to hunt and kill Jews?"

"I think many are afraid that if they don't hate and kill us, the Nazis will kill them."

After a while he stops, puts me down and we go for cover. We hear people speaking Russian. My cousin understands Russian. When they come closer, he talks to them. We find out they're Ukrainian. I'm afraid they're going to kill us, but they say they're partisans too and they fight any Nazis in their way. Because they were soldiers and still have guns, they can survive better than we do.

The leader says, "Don't worry. The war will be over soon and the Russians will save you."

CHAPTER 10:
THE BARN

THE WINTER OF 1943 isn't over. The cold is still unbearable. Uncle Yossef coughs all the time. He has trouble breathing. I'm getting too weak to run to the farms, so my cousins go to steal food without us.

On one of their raids, Ilya and Uri see a very large barn at a farm and discover enormous piles of hay inside. They agree on a plan to keep us safe and warm for a while.

The following night, the four of us go back to that farm. We choose the largest pile of hay in the back of the barn and clear out an opening that faces the rear of the building. It is large enough for my uncle and me to fit in. My cousins loosen a couple of boards next to us so they can sneak some food inside every few days.

Uncle Yossef says that we cannot talk at all during the day and only whisper at night. It's scary and my uncle has his arm around me and keeps it there the whole time we are sleeping the first night.

To help ease the boredom during the days, we try to exercise different parts of our body in this small space. First we take turns rubbing our legs and try to stretch them as far as they can go. We do the same thing with our arms. Then we roll our shoulders and move our heads from side to side. We blow out our cheeks and move our eyes around. My uncle looks so funny when he does this that it makes me laugh. He whispers "shhhh" but continues and I have to laugh to myself. I know he does this to amuse me. After dark, we creep out of our space and stand up and move around a little.

My cousins bring us food, and we take our time eating-taking small bites and chewing a long time before swallowing. We eat this way to get full quicker. Also it helps to kill the time.

To relieve ourselves, we do it as far away from where we sit as possible and cover it with fresh hay. At first, the smell is awful, but we get used to it.

The farmer comes into the barn every morning to get hay for his livestock. We hear the rustle of the hay as he takes some from the top of one of the piles. We don't move or even breathe until he leaves.

We live this way for many days and our bodies are stiff and cramped. Each time Ilya and Uri come, we ask how much longer. They say it will be soon and to keep our spirits up.

One night when my cousins come to bring us food, they see two German soldiers with guns walking around the barn. They wait until the soldiers are on the other side and crawl over to get us out through the loosened boards.

When we are safely on our way back to the woods, I ask, "How did they know we were there?" Ilya says, "Probably the farmer heard or more likely smelled something when he went in to get hay and suspected there were Jews hiding there."

"Why didn't he just tell us to get out?"

"He probably was afraid we had guns, so he reported it to the Nazis." "Then why didn't the soldiers get us."

"I don't think they knew how many of us they'd find

and were waiting for more soldiers to come. That's why we had to get out quick."

We can only imagine the Germans and the Polish farmers, who were German collaborators, tearing the barn apart and going through all the hay. My uncle says when they find only excrement in our hiding place, it will be a message to them. "No Jews for you this time. Only poop."

It's getting warmer, because it's near the end of winter, so we stay in the forest with the rest of the partisans. We are here through the summer. Ilya and Uri make their regular farm raids for food. We are not so hungry, because we're picking berries, nuts, crab apples and nuts again. But the constant diarrhea is back.

I'm at my lookout post. We move our shelter each time the Germans or Polish collaborators are near. I am happy to be around the campfire again and to see Tanya. She says she missed me and talks to me. I tell her what happened while I was away. She hugs me all the time. It feels good.

The summer passes very fast and winter is soon here again. It's 1944. I'm nine years old now. Uncle Yossef and I still can't stand the cold. Uri and Ilya take us to our family's long-time friend, Peter Gorski.

I ask uncle, "Will we be safe there? Remember what happened at the Yaskovich house."

"We must take a chance. Even though there are some Polish who are German collaborators, we owe our lives to many of our Polish friends. They put their lives in danger to help us."

"What about Yaskovich?"

"I'm not so sure Yaskovich would have given you up, but I am sure Peter Gorski will do everything he can to keep us safe. That's all we can ask him to do."

My cousins bring us to Peter Gorski 's house. The four of us go down to his basement and see three cots there. Peter Gorski says he is a member of the underground and has helped many Jews. His son provided the people who slept on these cots with false documents, and then they went to another shelter.

My uncle is happy to see his friend and thankful he will help us. Peter says he will give us passports. We'll receive them by the time we are ready to leave. Gorski shelters and feeds us for the rest of the winter, and he keeps us up to date on the progress of the War. He says that Germany is losing many battles and the Americans and the Russians are liberating most of the countries Germany occupied. He predicts the war will be over soon.

When the warm weather arrives, we leave to go back to the woods. Peter gives us enough money to last us for a while as well as food, clothing and false passports.

Uncle Yossef puts the money and passports safely in his money belt and hugs Peter Gorski. "I'll never forget you, my friend. You have saved our lives."

Again, we return to the forest and things are quiet for several months. We lost contact with the rest of our partisan group and hope they are safe. Until the cold weather arrives we have enough food. We're tired of this life. The only thing keeping us going is the knowledge that it will be over soon.

PART II:
THE POST WAR
YEARS

By July 1944, the battlefront was nearing Eishyshok
(Poland). A number of the surviving Jewish partisans
went off to join the advancing Red Army, eager to
fight the Germans openly and hasten the day of
liberation. But the promise of liberation brought
danger as well as hope to the few surviving Jews who
remained in hiding in the countryside. Even as the
earth beneath their feet rumbled to the rhythms of
the Russian army s approach, and the night skies lit
up with the long red arcs of the shells fired by the
Russian cannons, the Jews who had lived through the
horrors of the Holocaust wondered whether they
would live to see freedom. They feared they would
either be murdered by the AK (home army), who
were searching out the last Jews with renewed
intensity, or incinerated by one of the German or
Russian shells that were landing all around them.

*There Once Was A World, by Yaffa Eliach— Copyright
1998—(Little, Brown & Company), Pg. 655.*

CHAPTER 11:

LIBERATION

THE YEAR IS 1945. I'm ten years old. We hear a lot of gunfire. At first we think we're being hunted again, but no one comes. The guns get louder. When we see planes we know the war is over and the Russians are here. We run toward the fighting and get to a potato field. It's flat with no protection. We can hear shooting orders in both languages. The Russians shooting at Germans and Germans shooting at the Russians. We aren't sure what we should do. Are we safer in the forest with the Germans? Should we go over to the Russians?

My cousin Ilya says, "Remember when I spoke to the Ukrainian partisans, they said the war was almost over and they didn't kill us. Maybe the Russians won't kill Jews like the Germans or the Polish Jew hunters."

When Uri hears this, he says, "I'm going over to the Russian side."

Uncle Yossef says, "No, I'm not sure that would be wise. We need to talk about it."

"There's nothing to talk about. It can't be worse than it is here. I'm going." And he runs.

We have no choice but to follow him. We get caught in a potato field between the German and Russian armies. When we're strafed by diving airplanes, we drop to the ground and lie single file in order to make a narrow target.

After each time a plane dives and shoots, we tug at each other's ankles to see if the person in front is still alive. We slowly creep toward the other side and, finally, are "liberated" by the Russians.

CHAPTER 12:
KRAKOW

THE RUSSIANS DON'T welcome us with open arms. Two of the soldiers point guns at us and ask for identification. When Uncle Yossef explains we are Polish Jewish partisans and were hiding out in the woods, they're not impressed. One of them says, "Jews, huh?"

My uncle and cousins look at each other and then at me. Then Uncle Yossef thinks fast and says, "We have been trying to save this little Polish boy. His mother and father were killed by the Germans and he's all alone. We think he has relatives left in Poland. We want to help him find them."

At first I don't know what he's talking about, but then I know that Uncle wants me to play along. In Polish, one of the soldiers asks me. "Is that true, kid?" When I have trouble getting the word "Yes" out of my mouth because I stutter so much, he says, "Never mind. Go." We run fast toward Zasov and Uncle Yossef says, "The Russians aren't crazy about Jews either."

In Zasov, the whole village is war torn. The big house that belonged to the boss of the village is just a shell. Most of the houses are now rubble. People are running around looking for family. We go to where Uncle's house and my house used to be. We stand together and have tears in our eyes thinking of the lives we used to have and the loved ones who are dead. I wonder if my mother's candlesticks are still buried here somewhere.

A young woman is walking up the little hill. She looks very skinny. Her hair is thin and her eyes are sad and empty, but they come alive when she sees us. Uncle screams, "Thank God, it's Leah." She runs to us and we can't stop hugging and crying all at once.

After we calm down, we sit on the ground in a circle and Leah tells us what happened to her. She was in the concentration camp near Krakow the whole time. Very hard, but she met two new friends there, Ruth and Kerinka. They slept on either side of Leah. Ruth, a pretty dark-haired girl a little older than Leah and Kerinka, who had a bad cough, was so thin you could see her bones. The only time she smiled was when the three girls whispered to each other at night, talking about their old life, their families and their dreams of freedom. During the day, they worked in a nearby factory under guard and managed not to call attention to themselves.

Kerinka's cough was constant but she tried not to be too loud. She didn't want the guard to hear her. They had no use for sick prisoners. After returning from the factory one day, the three girls said good night to each other and fell asleep. The following morning, Leah and Ruth couldn't get Kerinka up. She was dead. They had no choice but to leave her there and went off to line up and go to work. When they returned, Kerinka was gone. The girls didn't talk about it that evening, but couldn't sleep. Instead they cried without making a sound and held hands.

One night, a guard came and took Ruth away. Leah became very worried when she didn't return. In the morning Ruth came back but didn't tell Leah anything. She changed after that and didn't talk a lot. Often she would stare off into the distance and not respond to any of Leah's questions.

When they were liberated from the concentration camp, they separated. Leah wanted to go to Zasov to try to find us and Ruth stayed in Krakow to find her family. They were both sad and happy. Sad because they had to say good-bye, but happy because they now had some hope for their future.

Leah keeps saying how lucky we are that our family found each other. We join hands, and walk around the town. Leah asks about her mother, Esther, her sister, Basha, and her Aunt Shanna, my mother. When we tell her they were all killed, she cries and pulls at her hair.

There is no place to stay in Zasov. The whole village is leveled, so we start walking toward Krakow. We don't care that we are tired and hungry. Our little family is together and we are free.

We get to Krakow and it looks better than Zasov. Thanks to Peter Gorski, we have enough money to rent a one-room flat in a 4-story tenement house with a very small kitchen and bathroom. It's in an old dilapidated building with most of the windows boarded up. It's crowded and there aren't enough beds, but it's cheap and we don't care. Uncle Yossef says, "Compared to the woods, this is a palace."

Our daily lives are much better now. I am happy that our family is together.

One morning I wake up with a terrible oozing rash. Because I am so undernourished, I'm a target for disease. I can't stand looking at this ugly rash, but Leah nurses me with compresses and is very gentle and caring. She reminds me of my mother. Her voice is soothing while she tends to me. After a week, I get better and am able to enjoy our little home and a taste of freedom.

But soon we learn that Poland is more anti-Semitic than ever. The Jews are shunned and hated not only by the Polish but by the Russians as well. There is no future for us here and we begin to plan ways to get out of Poland.

We are able to buy some food with the rest of the money Peter gave us and it keeps us going for a while. We are still hungry. Uncle Yossef, Ilya and Uri go out to see about getting work. Ilya and Uri return, drop the zlotys they made on the table and lay down to take a nap. When Uncle returns, he has large packages of cigarettes with him. He calls me over and whispers so the cousins won't overhear.

"Chiel, do you want to help me make some money?"

"Of course."

He gives me one of the packages of cigarettes and matches and takes me outside to the busy street.

"Now, stand up straight and smooth your hair. I want you to sell these cigarettes and matches. Don't forget to smile."

He tells me how much to charge. When I return and give Uncle the zlotys, he's pleased.

He trades the zlotys for Russian rubles and then

changes the rubles for dollars. He uses the dollars to buy American gold coins for our escape from Poland. After my cousins go to work I go out every day. I sell almost all of the cigarettes and am proud that I can help.

When I'm out trying to sell the last of the cigarettes, Ilya walks by and sees me. He's angry and pulls me home and yells at Uncle Yossef for sending me, a little boy, to do this.

Uncle Yossef, says, "Chiel is very brave and has been able to survive so far by being as strong and as smart as any of us."

That's the end of my cigarette business.

CHAPTER 13:
ZAKOPANE

THE IRON CURTAIN falls. We are stuck in Poland. Everyone hates us. The Polish, the Germans and now the Russians. It's very hard to get work. We have very little food.

My uncle tells me that one hundred orphaned survivors are being gathered and taken to the mountain resort town of Zakopane for rest and relaxation. I have a chance to be one of them. I don't want to go, but he insists because there's no food to speak of and I'm very run down. I' II just be away for a short time, then he'll come and get me.

I become one of the 100 orphans. It's a beautiful spot nestled at the bottom of the highest mountain range in the Carpathians. The group is traveling in two buses. I can breathe the clean air. My spirits are raised and I become excited as we approach the resort. I wish my family were here, but there are children everywhere. I'll be able to make new friends. We have a wonderful supper with a dessert of strawberries and cream.

The only problem is I get sick on the second day and spend months in the hospital recuperating from chickenpox and complications caused by my poor nutrition. I'm sent to a hospital run by nuns and they nurse me back to health.

Several months pass and I get well. Most of the other kids are gone. I'm one of the few who remain. There are a bunch of us who are healthy now, but no one comes. What's going to happen? We don't know.

Will we be here for the rest of our lives? Where is my uncle? He said he'd get me. Now, I'm really mad. The hell with him!

Zakopane is beautiful. We don't have enough clothes, so we wear hospital gowns all the time. Jewish and non-Jewish kids-all orphans who survived the war-play together. We run around the hospital grounds and have a good time.

The nuns like me and I'm crazy about them, so I start to help out. While I'm up on a ladder hanging up a picture of Jesus, one of the nuns asks me, "Chiel, have you thought about becoming a Christian?"

"Yes, but I really can't do it. I survived the war as a Jew. Many members of my family were killed because they were Jewish. To honor their memory, I must remain a Jew." The nuns understand and don't ask again.

My uncle finally comes to get me. I'm very angry, so I pretend I don't remember him. Even though I'm healthy, I stay in my bed with my eyes closed tight and groan. "I'm sick and have a fever. Who are you? Go away!" I turn my head to the wall.

"What are you talking about? I'm your Uncle Yossef" Then he comes closer to me and whispers, "I know you're upset that you've been here so long, but we were starving and weren't able to give you any food. I knew you'd be taken good care of here. We're suffering just as much under the Russians as the Poles and Germans. They hate us. We must leave Poland. I want you to come with me and we'll make a plan together."

When I hear this, I jump out of bed, get my one change of clothes and prepare to go back to Krakow with him.

In Krakow, my cousins are happy to see me. They look much thinner and the apartment seems smaller than I remember. There are rolls of leather everywhere. My uncle says he was able to buy this leather in the black market and will be able to sell it for profit. Then we'll have enough money to get us out of Poland.

Before I fall asleep at night, I like the strong smell of leather. It reminds me we'll be able to leave.

We spend the next day together. Walking, talking, shopping and planning. Tired after waiting in long lines to buy bread, milk and cheese, we come back to our place to find that all the leather is gone. Someone must have been watching and stole it right after we left. Not only was the leather stolen, but the passports Peter Gorski gave us are gone too. The only one left is my Uncle's. He kept his with the money in his money belt. The others were hidden in the room. The thieves found them.

My uncle is so upset, he says he needs to go for a walk and think. I ask, "Can I come?" "All right. But be quiet."

We go to the market square and stare at the kiosks and the people selling their wares. "Uncle Yossef, will we ever be able to get out of Poland?"

"I think we will, Chiel. Even though everything seems

to be working against us and we have no money and no future. We must not give up hope. God will provide."

A Russian officer is looking over some knitted scarves and picks one up. He sees us and in Yiddish tells my uncle he speaks very little Polish and asks to please find out how much the scarf costs. After Uncle Yossef asks and tells him the price, we start to walk away.

After the officer pays, he catches up with us. "Thank you for doing that. Would you both like to join me for coffee and cake?"

My mouth starts to water when I think of eating cake and Uncle Yossef sees me nodding my head up and down. He says, "I think we'd like that."

We walk to the closest food stand and Uncle asks, "How did you know I'm a Jew?" "I didn't. I took a guess."

Over coffee, he says his name is Dimitri Yacova and his mother often spoke to him in Yiddish. She was a Jew and his father a Catholic. They didn't observe either religion. He was told not to acknowledge his mother's religion because of all the antisemitism in Russia. He joined the Russian Army at a young age. Although he loves his country, he's upset with their present government and the way the Jews are treated. He is married with a family and misses them very much. He bought the scarf for his daughter. My uncle invites him to come to our little apartment with us. Before they leave the square, Dimitri buys some pastry treats for our family.

When my cousins see a Russian officer enter our apartment they get scared. Uri asks, "What's this about? Are we being arrested?"

Uncle Yossef says, "Don't worry. He's a friend."

We serve tea and eat the pastries Dimitri brought us as

we listen to the story of his life in Russia. After uncle tells him what we've been through, he says he'd like to help us, but it will take a few days to plan.

He stays for a week and likes being with us. We remind him of his own family. It's crowded in our small apartment, but Dimitri doesn't mind sleeping on the floor. He says it's more comfortable than in other places he slept.

He and Uncle rise early and take walks. Uncle helps Dimitri practice his Polish and they have long discussions. They become good friends and, for once, we have enough food. It's nice to have full bellies again. We would like to have Dimitri with us all the time. He says he can't but will stay until he finds a way to smuggle us out of Poland.

We feel very lucky to have Dimitri in our lives.

CHAPTER 14:
DIMITRI

D IMITRI STAYS FOR six days and nights. He buys food for us every day. Though the antisemitism in Krakow is terrible, having Dimitri with us raises our spirits. One day we all go to the market square. Dimitri sees a camera for sale at one of the kiosks and buys it. He takes our pictures to show his family. We want to have pictures of him too, so he orders two copies of the prints made.

Each time he and Uncle Yossef return from their long walks, they are very excited. On the seventh day, Dimitri calls us all together and says he and Uncle Yossef have devised a plan to smuggle us out of Poland. He says to go about our business today as we always do. Tonight, layer our clothing and put any other items we think necessary in our pockets, but do not carry anything. He will be the only one holding a bag with several bottles of whiskey. Then we will all take a long walk in groups of two. He'll be with Leah, I with Uncle Yossef and Uri and Ilya together. We are to talk about unimportant things, so we will not arouse suspicion by the people we see along the way.

Dimitri was able to get hold of an army truck and he loaded it with empty oil barrels. He left it camouflaged at the side of the road on the way to the Czech border.

When we reach the truck, each one of us must crawl into an empty oil barrel and stay quiet until he gets us out.

I feel very excited, but I am not afraid. I think back at all the times we were out in the open, running for our lives. This isn't as bad. We all agree it's an excellent plan.

Dimitri goes out to purchase the whiskey, and pick up our pictures. We look through our flat and gather as many clothes as we can wear. Leah is very thin and puts many layers on. Then she parades around the room with her hands on her hips pretending she's a model. When Uri and Ilya see this, they do the same and Uri ties one of Leah's kerchiefs under his chin, grabs Ilya and they dance around the room. I hold my side because I'm laughing so much. Uncle Yossef just says, "Hmmmmm, Hmmmm," and gives us a little smile. We are all in a good mood because we will be running again and, this time, we see some hope for our future.

After dark, Dimitri and Leah start out first. He is dressed in his Captain's uniform. After a few minutes, Ilya and Uri walk a few paces behind them. Then Uncle Yossef and me. It's a clear night and we have Dimitri well in our sights. We don't walk too slow or too fast. I overhear Ilya and Uri talk about the beautiful carvings they saw at the market square that afternoon. Ilya used to carve figures out of wood and appreciates all the work it takes to complete a figure.

Uncle asks me if I remember how we used to fish with his hand-made fishing rod. He points out the bright stars on this clear and beautiful night. I tell him about the time I tried to catch a falling star.

We can't hear Dimitri and Leah up ahead, but we see

him and the Babushka on Leah's head nodding up and down as Dimitri is talking to her.

I look at the buildings in Krakow, some of them untouched by the war. Still beautiful. I think it's too bad that we're so hated. This could have been a nice place to live. Again, I feel that tinge of guilt that I couldn't save my mother. I wish she could be here. It's getting darker and I'm tired. I wonder how much longer we have to walk. I see a truck up ahead.

Dimitri tells us to crawl into the oil barrels. Then he gets in the front and starts to drive. The oil barrels are small and uncomfortable. They smell and jiggle up and down as we ride on the road. The truck stops at the first border to Czechoslovakia. We hear the guard talking to Dimitri in Polish. My heart is thumping. I stay very still and say a silent prayer.

"What are you carrying, Captain?" "Just some oil barrels."

"I have to look."

Dimitri takes out a bottle of whiskey and gets out of the truck and says, "Of course. But first, you must be tired. How about a drink to keep you going?"

The guard hesitates for a moment. "Thanks."

Dimitri hands him the bottle and some folded money. After the guard takes a drink, he starts to hand it back to him.

Dimitri says, "No, you keep it. Do you want to look in the back now?" "Nah! It's okay."

"Have a nice night."

Whew! We are through the first border. Now we're on our way to the East Berlin border.

We hear the same conversation with the East Berlin

guard, but this time he checks the back of the truck. My heart skips a beat. I hold my breath. Again. When the guard says, "Okay," Dimitri gets back in and drives for a while. He stops, comes in back and waits before saying anything. We stay still. I wonder if something is wrong. Then Dimitri says, "You can get out now."

We can't hold back a victory yell and climb out of the barrels and jump down off the truck. We take turns hugging Dimitri. When Uncle Yossef gives him an extra hug and kisses him on both cheeks, Dimitri presses a package of our photos in his hand.

After our excitement dies down, we must say good-bye to our friend. Dimitri wishes us good luck, gets behind the wheel and drives away.

CHAPTER 15:
EAST GERMANY

THE YEAR IS 1946. It's early morning. We've been walking around East Berlin. Because the Germans destroyed so many Jewish lives during the War, we're happy to see the city in complete ruins. Bridges are rubble and the buildings destroyed.

The Russian soldiers act like savages. They take over the streets, rape the German women, and abuse German citizens in every way. We keep walking and feel some satisfaction that this East German city is a mess.

Some young German teenagers come toward us. They look, point, hold their noses and cross the street. Shortly after that we see a young couple cross the street too. It's obvious that the German citizens are now as downtrodden as we are, but it doesn't excuse the way they react to us. We're glad that they're suffering too.

We pass a few Russian soldiers who laugh and say some things in Russian. My cousin, Ilya, says they're making fun of the way we're dressed and call us dirty Jews. We really are dirty from our long trip in the oil barrels. They start to follow us and keep laughing and making remarks. Uncle Yossef and I ignore them, but Ilya and Uri glance at each other, ready to fight. We're relieved when the soldiers just continue walking.

It's good to be out of Poland, but this Soviet-controlled East Berlin isn't any better. I wonder what our people did to be treated so badly by so many people. Uncle Yossef refuses to be discouraged and says there has to be a way to get someplace where we can be free. We are growing more and more uncomfortable in East Berlin. We have to get out of here and into the Western zone fast.

We spot a trolley station ahead with people waiting to board. Uncle leaves us to ask a young woman among them where the trolley is going.

When he returns he says, "It goes to West Berlin."

I know West Berlin is under Western control, so I say, "Let's take the trolley."

"It's not that easy, Chiel. There's a border we must cross. There are five of us with only one passport."

We continue talking. Uri says, "Let's go anyway and take our chances."

Uncle frowns. "What's the matter with you? Do you want to get arrested by the Russians?" Ilya agrees with Uncle. "Maybe we can find someone to make up some fake passports."

Uncle says, "Where? And anyway, we don't have any extra money for that, and we don't have enough time. It's not safe to stay in the Eastern sector too long. The Russians are animals and before you know it, they might make up some excuse to arrest us."

As we are talking, we notice the trolleys going back and forth. There are street urchins, laughing, talking to each other, hanging on to the outside of the trolley and taking a free ride. The Russian soldiers, who have guns, wave to the kids and joke with them.

Uncle Yossef is looking at this and rubs his chin.

"Hmmmmm, Hmmmmm. We're going to West Germany and we're gonna use Chiel. This is perfect for him."

After a long discussion about how we'll pull this off, a decision is made.

We check out the people boarding the trolley. Then we look at ourselves. If we get on the trolley the way we are now, it's certain we'll arouse suspicion. We need to dress more like everyone else. The rest rooms are nearby. Uncle tells us to go in one at a time and clean ourselves up.

When Leah comes out, she looks much better. She washed up, her hair is combed and she took off the dirty layer of clothes. Her dress is a little wrinkled, but she looks pretty good. Uri is next. He comes out with his hair slicked back, his face and clothes clean. Ilya and Uncle take their turn and are improved too. When I am about to go in the rest room, they tell me not to clean up. I have to look like a poor street kid. I don't mind, because I'm comfortable when I'm dirty.

Uncle Yossef says, "Wait for my signal."

We wait for the trolley to unload the passengers. Then he nods his head. I run to the back of the trolley and hang on. I blend in with the other dirty kids pretty well. Uncle Yossef boards and shows his passport. After he gets over the West Berlin border, he gets out. I jump off as he steps down, so he can slip the passport to me. I return to East Berlin and give Ilya Uncle's passport.

Ilya uses the pictures Dimitri gave us and cuts them up. He finds one of Uri and replaces Uncle Yossef's picture. Uri takes it and boards. I jump back on the trolley and, on this ride, I hope Uri doesn't try to prove he's brave by trying something foolish. I pray he gets through all right. My prayers are answered.

When we arrive in West Berlin, I jump off the trolley, run to Uri and he sneaks the passport to me. I skip back to the side of the trolley, hang on and ride back to return it to Ilya. He needs to put Leah's picture on now. He hopes the Russians won't know that it's a man's name. We wait for the next trolley. Leah steps on. I jump on the back and pray Leah will be okay. My prayers are answered again. At the station, she gives me the passport. I come back, give it to Ilya, and he puts on his own picture before he boards the next trolley. I jump on for the last time.

When I join my family in West Berlin, they praise me, pat my back and give me a hug. Uri says, "I hate to say this, but Chiel is our new hero."

I am so excited! I wasn't scared at all.

I love doing stuff like this.

CHAPTER 16

AUSTRIA

THE YEAR IS 1946. After we arrive in the American zone of occupation in West Berlin, we are dispatched to Austria and are placed in a hotel with 300 other survivors. It's located in Bad Ischl—a beautiful resort town near Salzburg in the foothills of the Alps. The hotel serves as a Jewish DP camp. Wherever we look, we see a view of the mountains. It reminds me of the time I spent in Zakopane in Poland only now I'm not sick. The air is crisp and clean and again, I think of my mother and that nagging feeling of guilt is back. How she would love the beauty here.

Ruth, Leah's friend from the concentration camp, is at the hotel. After they have a wonderful reunion, Leah introduces her to us. She is very pretty. She smiles at me and musses my hair.

Leah and Ruth spend hours talking and laughing together. I think Ruth likes me, but she likes Ilya too. One evening, before bedtime, I'm dragging a stick along the iron fence outside the hotel. I see Ilya and Ruth walking up ahead. They are talking and when they stop, Ilya kisses her. I turn around and run into the hotel. I'm jealous of Illya. I wish I were grown up, so I could kiss Ruth.

Leah has a boyfriend too. He's another survivor at Bad Ischl. His name is Ben and he's crazy about her. At first, she doesn't care for him so much, but after he insists that one day he will marry her and he'll become very rich, she starts to like him more. Now they sit together at meals. They act silly, and stare into each other's eyes.

Every day I go out on the street to watch the American soldiers playing catch with gloves and a baseball. A black soldier throws me a glove and says, "Wanna play?"

It's the first time I've ever seen a black person. I'm scared at first, but he has a friendly smile, "Okay."

I like the soldier and I like playing catch. Soon I'm pretty good at it.

In the surrounding apartment houses, Austrian women hang out of the windows. The American soldiers throw chocolate bars and stockings up to them. Then the soldiers go up to their apartments. If I had some chocolates or stockings to throw, I'd like to go to their apartments too, but I'm not old enough.

I'm sick of seeing Leah and Ben together and jealous of my cousin Ilya. So when I walk by a house next to the hotel and notice a little girl with a big bow in her hair, I want to talk to her, but I keep walking. A couple of houses down, I see a red wagon out in front and take it. When I roll it back to see the girl I point to myself and say, "Chiel."

She points to herself and says, "Hilde."

I push the wagon toward her and she jumps in.

We spend all day playing and when I come back, my uncle asks where I got the wagon. When I tell him, he says, "We do not steal unless it's food to keep us alive. Return it. NOW!"

At first the Austrians are sympathetic towards the Jewish survivors. It doesn't last. The Americans are stationed here in Austria to protect us, but we are confronted with hate everywhere. There is graffiti on synagogues and many demonstrations against us.

We are fed well, but my stomach is small and I can't eat a lot. Leah always sits with me after everyone leaves to get me to finish. Sometimes I'm slow on purpose, so Leah will pay attention to me. One night after dinner when Leah is sitting and coaching me to eat, we hear chanting outside. "Beat the Jews to death—lynch the swines." A couple of bricks fly through the window. Leah and I dive under the table. The Austrian police break up the crowd, only because the windows are broken. They don't care about the hateful demonstration.

I ask Uncle Yossef, "Why is antisemitism still everywhere?"

"People don't change. The Austrians are worse than the Germans. Now they blame the Jewish survivors for everything that goes wrong in their country. That's why we will go to America. We'll be free and treated like everybody else. It won't be perfect, but a lot better."

I'm the only child here. Most of the children my age were killed in concentration camps. Very few survived the war. Although hard, kids like me had a better chance of survival as partisans in the forest. All the adults in the hotel watch over me. I'm their mascot.

The manager tells us we will be evicted. They don't want displaced persons and Jews in the hotel. We hear they're going to take away all of our valuables. They make a rule saying Jews are not allowed to have anything of value in their possession. All of the people here have items to help them survive. We're determined not to let the Austrians take anything else from us.

Uncle Yossef calls me into a meeting. "Chiel, you need to help us out again."

He puts a large coat on me and loads me up with everyone's watches, rings, bracelets and other valuables, stuffing them in the pockets and lining of the coat. It's hard for me to walk. I waddle from side to side, but I manage to go outside. I take a baseball with me, walk around for a while and then sit down. I keep throwing the ball up and down. Some people walk by me and smile. When I see Ilya coming for me, I know I can come back. They're gone. Our things are safe. When I return to the hotel, I hear clapping and I walk straighter with my chin up. It feels good to hear the cheering. Even better than being a lookout in the woods.

Everyone is angry at the Austrians and we want to take revenge somehow. Uncle Yossef calms us down, "No. Revenge isn't the answer. We will go to the American authorities and tell them what's going on here."

It works. They say they'll take us out of the hotel and move us into the Schonbrunn Palace which is where King Franz Josef spent his summers. We Jews who survived the concentration camps and the ghettos and living like animals in the woods are now going to live in a palace. No one believes it.

When the Americans come to get us, we think it's a joke. We'll probably be staying in another hotel.

CHAPTER 17

KING JOSEF'S PALACE

I WALK THROUGH the doors of the palace. Am I in a dream? The beauty everywhere is unbelievable. Crystal chandeliers, parquet floors, mirrored walls and an outdoor swimming pool that can be covered and changed to a dance floor. The grounds are dotted with nut and fruit trees . There are band concerts in the evenings. It takes us more than a week to discover everything and to realize we are living here.

When I first arrive, I think about my mother again, remembering the fairy tales she read to me. I feel she watches me enjoying myself.

From my room, I see a peach tree outside my window. I reach out and pluck an unripened peach. It's hard as a rock, but the idea that I can do this is amazing. We aren't hungry for a change. The American Jewish organizations send us food and we get CARE Packages from relatives in the United States.

Being with this group is like having a big family. I'm undernourished and skinny, and because I can't eat very much at one time, people keep trying to feed me. The atmosphere is loving. For once I am very happy.

In the spring of 1946, we hold our first Passover service since the liberation. Uncle Yossef and I bake matzos in an enormous palace kitchen. He does most of the work. I help by running back and forth following Uncle's orders. He explains everything as he works. We purify the dishes in boiling water. The CARE Packages from America contain some favorite Passover foods. Uncle Yossef talks the American authorities into getting us kosher wine and chickens so we can have chicken soup, baked chicken and hard-boiled eggs. All the women pitch in to help. We prepare a delicious meal.

The dining hall is wonderful: white tablecloths, candles and flowers. The table set with china dishes, silver, wine and the Seder Plate holds all the symbolic foods. We are dressed in whatever *best* clothes we have. Uncle Yossef appears very important as he conducts the Seder in a white prayer shawl and yarmulke.

Uncle starts reading about Passover from a book called the Haggadah, and the women bring out the food.

The youngest person in the group traditionally asks the Passover four questions, so Uncle Yossef looks at me. I start with "Why is this night different from all other nights?"

Uncle Yossef answers, "Passover celebrates the release of the Jews from the land of Egypt. Our forefathers were slaves to Pharaoh. The last years we were slaves to Hitler. This year we are free. Blessed be He who has brought us forth from oppression."

This is my best Passover ever.

We don't work. We just wait to go to America. But until that happens, we have a wonderful time. We play soccer games. I'm a goalie.

Ilya and Ruth fall in love. They're always together. I see them giggling, hugging and kissing. I now know I never had a chance with Ruth, but she likes me and musses my hair. Uncle Yossef says, "Ilya, it's time you got married. This is a perfect place for a wedding."

And it is. The chuppah *(canopy)* is set up in one of the large rooms. Ruth looks like a princess, wearing a beautiful dress that one of the other survivors loaned her. Ilya and Ruth stand under the chuppah and the rabbi recites the blessing. They each sip from the same cup of wine and then exchange vows. Ilya places a ring on Ruth's finger. They both sip the wine again. Then Ilya puts the glass on the floor and crushes it with his foot. This is a symbol of destroying the sadness that mingles with happiness in human life. Everybody shouts mazel tov. Ilya and Ruth kiss as husband and wife. We all clap.

For the reception, the swimming pool is covered and there is dancing after the ceremony. The bride and groom dance first. Then one of the men in the group dances the Kazatsky, a Russian peasant dance. Ruth and Ilya are hoisted up on chairs as king and queen of the night while we all sing and dance around them.

We have many kinds of foods. Best of all, at last we have something to celebrate. Ruth and Ilya are so happy. It's a turning point in all our lives. An end and a beginning. The end of the terrible times we have all suffered, but the beginning of a better future with hope and happiness.

My contentment is short lived. One day in January 1947 my Uncle Yossef comes out to the field where I am playing soccer.

"Come in Chiel. I want to talk to you."

"What is it uncle? I'm in the middle of a game." "You can come back out. C'mon with me."

When we're alone, he tells me that one thousand Jewish survivors from all over Europe will be given a chance to go to America. My heart dropped. "What does that have to do with me?"

"Since you are an orphan and have an aunt and uncle in Boston who want to adopt you, you'll be able to go on the next ship."

"But I don't know them. I want to stay here with you."

"Chiel, you don't have a choice. You have to take this opportunity. I don't know when we'll be able to go to America."

"I don't care. I'll wait."

"There's a quota system. We don't know when we'll go. But when we get there, we'll all see each other. In the meantime, we'll write letters and let you know what's going on."

"I'm not going."

"You're going. It's for your own good. You have to go."

I know my uncle. No use arguing when he makes up his mind. I'll show him. He'll be sorry he's sending me away.

I dance around with one foot. "Okay, I can't wait. How soon can I leave?"

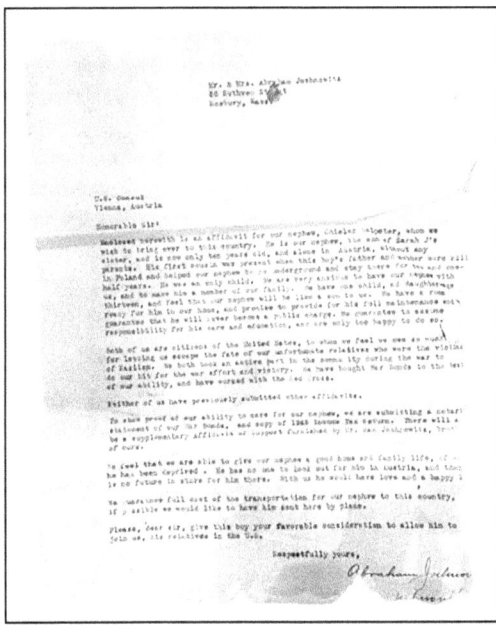

CHAPTER 18:
GOING TO AMERICA

I AM SO angry at my uncle I hardly speak to him. All the others know I have to leave and they tell me how much they'll miss me. This makes me sad.

Terrible nightmares now start to interrupt my sleep. Dogs with enormous teeth growl and chase me. I wake up just before they eat me.

Why can't I wait and go to America with my uncle and cousins? I understand about the quota, but I want to stay with them.

We're a family unit and we care for and protect each other. I won't know who I am without them.

I think of everything we've gone through. The ghetto, the escape from the camp, living in the woods. How I acted as a lookout when I was little. How I helped get

us here. We did everything together. We had meetings to decide what to do next. Why couldn't we have a meeting to decide whether or not I should go to America? They're my only family. I love them so much. Why do they want to get rid of me? Will I ever see them again?

The palace isn't so wonderful now. My stutter is worse. I try not to talk. Ruth sees me by myself sitting on the grass. "Chiel, let's talk."

I don't answer. She has a pad of paper and pencils with her. "I'm going to teach you how to write your name."

She musses my hair. "When you're in America you should be able to write something in English."

I don't care about writing my name. I don't say anything as she hands me a pencil. She writes and tells me to copy. I see she's not going to give up, so I copy what she wrote.

She kisses me on the cheek. "Very good! Now, let me teach you the alphabet."

After I repeat the letters and learn them, Ruth says when I get to America, I can go to school and learn to read and write. Then she musses my hair again and says she's proud of me. I don't feel good. I just wish I had time for her to teach me more.

My uncle gives me pictures of the aunt and uncle who are going to adopt me, then tells me about my American family.

I have two aunts in America. One lives in Boston and the other one lives in New York. The Boston aunt wants to adopt me. Her name is Sadie. In the photograph she looks very much like my mother. She and her husband went to America just after the war started. My uncle was in a concentration camp and had been tortured there. At the beginning of the war, the Jews had the option of buying themselves out of the camps, so he gave the guards most of his money, then he and my aunt came to America.

My other aunt, Vera, and her family arrived in America before the war started. They have a successful business and send us all the CARE packages we enjoy.

"Chiel, these are your mother's sisters, just as your Aunt Esther was. Remember how you loved her? You won't be alone. They'll take good care of you and love you."

Uncle Yossef gives me little presents for them. "When you enter their homes, give them these." "I won't know what to say to them, Uncle."

"Chiel, I know you're unhappy to be leaving us. I wish you could stay, but not only am I your uncle, I'm your Godfather. I have an obligation to do the best thing for you. I'll miss you every day. We went through a lot together. I'll always love you. And, don't forget, we will see each other again when we are all in America."

"It won't be the same without you."

"It will be better. You'll see."

Uri and Ilya tell me how much they'll miss me and Uri teases me about how he used to fool around with me. He says he remembers when I paid him back by passing him the worse burnt potatoes.

Ilya reminds me how he used to hoist me up on his shoulders when I got tired of running. I want to tell him I'm tired of running now. Why won't anyone help me?

Leah still sits with me and coaches me to eat. She says it will be easier to eat more in America. They have tastier food.

I know they're trying to make me feel better. I want to cry all the time. What's in store for me? I don't want to leave my life.

There is a big goodbye party the day before I leave. The last time we had a big party was Ilya's and Ruth's wedding. Today isn't as happy. Each person kisses me and wishes me well. They all say they will miss their "mascot." We became very close. I know I will always remember them.

On the day I have to leave, it's a cold winter day. I'm dressed in a warm coat and a hat with ear flaps. I'm not comfortable in the coat, but it will keep me warm. A car comes to pick me up. A little girl is in the car. My family hugs me one last time, then my uncle says, "Get in the car."

I pick up my leg, jump and dance around the car saying, "I'm going to America, yaay, I'm going to America!"

Leah starts to cry. Uncle Yossef says, "Remember our talk, Chiel. Soon, we'll all be together."

So I get in the car and start my trip. The girl's name is Becky. She is sniffling, tears running down her face, but I will not cry.

CHAPTER 19

THE SHIP

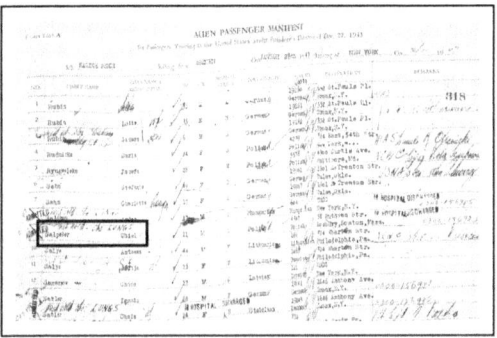

T HE MARINE PERCH is leaving from Bremen Harbor on January 28, 1947. I am almost twelve years old.

I wait for the ship in a building where there are barracks and the other orphans. The last time I was in Germany, we were running away from Poland. First by truck, then by trolley car. Now I'm back. This time I'll be getting away on a ship.

Becky is in the next bed and she keeps crying. "I'm afraid. I don't know anyone in America. I'll be all alone."

I'm sort of sorry for her. "No, you won't be alone. You'll probably be in an orphanage. There'll be lots of kids there."

She can't stop crying. I'm mad anyway and, with her

keeping me up, I get even madder. I tell her to shut the hell up, but she doesn't stop. I don't feel sorry for her anymore. I have to take my anger out on someone, so I grab Becky's blanket and throw it on the floor. Then I get my suitcase and run out into the snow in the middle of the night.

I feel better, because I'm running. That's what I do best. I cry and scream into the wind. Why am I being sent away? I know God is punishing me, because I wished my father dead, and the dogs killed him. Then I left my mother to die. But Uncle Yossef said that wasn't my fault, and says he loves me. So why am I being sent away? I don't understand. I throw my aunts' pictures and the gifts for them in the snow.

The authorities find me and bring me back to the barracks. The following day Becky won't talk to me, but I don't care. I board the ship with the rest of the 1,000 people. It's very cold. I hate wearing a hat. I'm still uncomfortable in my coat, but it's better than wearing rags in freezing weather.

The food on the ship is okay, but I don't have much of an appetite so I eat next to nothing. I have a bad cough and a headache. I miss Leah and think about her sitting with me while I ate. There is a storm at sea and the ship rocks back and forth. A lot of the kids are throwing up. It smells everywhere. When the rocking stops, I get away from the smell and walk on the lower deck. We're not allowed to wander around, but the crew is busy helping the sick kids and no one sees me. I hear talking and laughing up ahead. It's coming from one of the cabins. I walk by and peek in. Three kids are playing cards. They see me. "C'mon in. What's your name?"

They're friendly, so I go in. "Chiel." "Chiel, can you play Oko?"

I silently thank Uri for teaching me. "Sure, I play." "Do you have any money?"

Before I answer, I think about the money my uncle gave me for an emergency. They think they can win from me, but I'm a pretty good player. I decide to risk it. "Yes, I've got some money."

"Sit down."

The trip now becomes interesting. I sit down and play. The kids introduce themselves.

Sammy is 15 years old. Both his parents were killed at the beginning of the war. His mother was shot in a ghetto. Then his father got Sammy to a nun who'd been visiting the ghetto. She hid him in a convent until the end of the war. His father died in a work camp.

Joshua, who's 14, was hidden by a Polish neighbor before his parents were taken to Treblinka, a concentration camp. They both died there.

Jarek is 14. He too was a partisan in the woods. Both his parents were killed while they were running away.

I told them about my experiences. Sammy says, "You're lucky." "Lucky? Why?"

"Because you still have some family left."

After hearing the other stories, I do begin to feel lucky. Maybe it's not fair to blame my uncle. He did the right thing, trying to take care of me by sending me to a safe country where they don't hate Jews so much. I'll be able to go to school and no one will call me kike. I'll learn to read and write like Ruth said I would. Maybe my aunt will love me like my mother did. Maybe my new father will treat me better than my real one. I decide to tell Uncle Yossef I'm sorry when I see him again.

We play cards every day after that. I win eleven dollars by the end of the trip. I feel good about myself

The last day of our voyage, I'm playing cards with my new friends, when we hear a distress whistle followed by instructions to come to the upper deck. We throw our cards down and run up. All of the orphans are gathered together and told to put on life jackets.

A man is handing out the life jackets. I ask, "What's going on?"

"Because of the storm, there is some damage to the ship. To be on the safe side, we are being prepared."

I hear the blowing of the ship's whistles and I'm not so sure I believe this is not serious. Am I going to drown? All the kids are crying and shrieking. My new friends and I stay together.

Sammy, the oldest, says, "Don't worry, we didn't make it this far to have it end like this. I know we'll be okay." He sounds like an adult and we feel a lot better.

I later hear that a hunk of the ship fell off.

The ship arrives in New York Harbor. We have survived once again. In the distance, we see the Statue of Liberty. We dock at Ellis Island on February 11, 1947.

CHAPTER 20

ELLIS ISLAND

A T ELLIS ISLAND, the medical personnel checks us out. My hacking cough is worse. A young doctor is called to examine me. While he listens to my chest, he looks very serious and orders X-rays to be taken. I'm told to sit and wait until the X-rays are read. Then the doctor tells me I have tuberculosis and can't leave Ellis Island.

I cry and scream. "What do you mean? This is crazy. I hate America! It's no better here. I want to go back to Austria. Send me back to my family in Austria."

They say, "No that's impossible. You have to stay here."

I don't understand. I tell them I'm to be adopted by my aunt and uncle and live with them. They tell me my relatives will be notified, but I can't leave the island because I have a contagious disease

They put me in a hospital facility. I don't know what's going on. I'm scared out of my wits, because I'm thrown in a mental ward with a bunch of babbling patients. I can't speak English and I'm stuck in this place. I try to tell the nurses, I'm not crazy, but I speak in Polish and stutter, so they think I'm babbling too.

At night I wake to hear a voice and see a man in a white johnny dancing and singing up and down the ward. I must be having another nightmare.

My Aunt Sadie and Uncle Josh, who live in Boston,

are in touch with the authorities and they try to get me released, but can't. They call my Aunt Vera, who lives in New York to help. Aunt Vera is a member of a Jewish charitable organization. She knows Sylvia Weinstein Sullivan, who is also a member of this organization and the wife of Ed Sullivan, a famous American television variety show host. My aunt tells Sylvia Sullivan my story. She asks Mrs. Sullivan if she would use her influence to inquire and find out if I really have TB and how I can be released. So it turns out that Ed Sullivan's wife gets the doctors to recheck me. My cough is better, and they find out I don't have TB. At last, I'm free.

After Ellis Island, they send me to an orphanage in Yonkers, New York to wait for my paperwork to clear. I don't know where I am. I'm suspicious when we must line up to walk in. Miserable memories surface of bad treatment of people who were made to wait in lines. I'm afraid this will be the same.

But I'm wrong. Soon after we arrive, I begin to love this orphanage. I don't want to go anywhere else. The food is good. Every day we have milk and cookies for snacks. I eat my first orange. It has the most sweet and delicious taste I ever had. There are lots of kids to hang around with. It's fun. Each room holds six boys. My roommates are friendly. They show me where the baseball field is outside. In the building, kids work at printing, carpentry, arts and crafts and musical study.

In the gym, there's exercise equipment as well as a ping-pong table. I learn to play and become a good player. I slam the ball with one hand while holding my pants up with the other. The social work ladies watch me and clap every time I score. They praise me. No one calls me names. My Uncle Yossef was right. It's better in America.

After a couple of weeks, the administrator of the orphanage calls me into her office. She says my Aunt Sadie and Uncle Josh are coming to take me to live with them in Boston

My Uncle Yossef told me about them and that was his plan for me. But now I decide I don't want to go to Boston. I don't want to be adopted. As usual, I run away. This time, into the streets of New York. I don't know my way around so when I see a bus terminal, I hide there. The police are called. They find me and bring me back to the orphanage.

I'm sitting in the dormitory I share with five other boys. A staff member brings Uncle Josh into the room and introduces him to me and the other boys. My uncle says hello, then looks at the floor. He says it's dirty here and picks up a broom standing in the corner. He sweeps the floor. I'm embarrassed. The boys leave. Uncle Josh tries to talk to me. He is very nervous and his eye twitches. He says my Aunt Sadie couldn't come because she hurt her back. She was on her feet cooking all day for our Friday night meal and she can't wait to see me. He says he has a window cleaning business and wants me to work with him someday. Then he doesn't say anything.

I feel I have to break the silence. "Do you have a ping-pong table?" "No, why?"

"Because I'm a good player. They call me the champion."

When he says, "Maybe we can buy you one," I know he has no idea what a ping-pong table is. He says it's time to leave. Goes to my drawer and packs clothes in my suit-case.

We take a taxi to the train station. While we are riding on the train to Boston, my uncle sits staring straight ahead. I see this isn't going to work. This man doesn't know anything about children. I miss my Uncle Yossef more than ever.

CHAPTER 21:
MY NEW FAMILY

M Y NEW UNCLE and I arrive at his house in Roxbury, Massachusetts, a suburb of Boston. My Aunt Sadie is waiting for me. She greets us at the door. When I see how much she looks like my mother, I give her a big hug. Her arms remain at her sides, and she gives me a light kiss on the cheek. I'm disappointed but the delicious cooking smells reach my nostrils and I feel hungry. I remember my mother telling me what a good cook her sister is. Their house is warm and cheerful and my aunt has a nice smile. My uncle tries to make me feel at home, but he's still self-conscious.

It's Friday night. Aunt Sadie puts on a kerchief and after she blesses the candles, she gets busy bringing food to the table. We sit down to a wonderful meal of chopped liver, chicken soup, lettuce and tomatoes, pot roast and potatoes. I eat everything except the tomatoes. They remind me of the ones that grew outside of our outhouse in Zasov. Then she puts out a big bowl of fruit. I really love fruit. Maybe there's hope after all.

At first, I spend most of the days with my aunt. I watch her cook and help her around the house. She takes me shopping and when I see fruit my mouth waters. She smiles and buys as many kinds as they have. She speaks to me in Polish and in English-to help me get used to the language. She tells me about her childhood with my mother and my Auntie Esther and about her life after she married Uncle Josh.

They lived in Vienna before the war and owned a perfume store. They had a good life and many friends until the start of the war when Uncle Josh was taken off to a concentration camp. After that, no one was friendly to my aunt. She was alone in a hostile city.

In those early days of the war, my uncle was able to buy his way out of the camp. But the Nazis did a job on him, hitting him in the head over and over again with truncheons. It left him mentally scarred for life.

When my uncle got out of the camp, he and my aunt left for America. He had family here and they helped him start up a cleaning service. Not as pleasant as his perfume store, but my uncle was a hard worker and his new business became profitable.

So, I'm in this strange country, in a house with a cold aunt and a mentally disturbed uncle. They're very good people, but they have their own problems and don't understand mine. This is hard for me to get used to. After my mother died, Uncle Yossef became my parent. I miss his love and kindness.

My nightmares are horrible. German shepherds chase me every night. They are at my heels and I run until my heart is ready to burst. Just as they're about to eat me, I scream and wake up in a wet bed. I stay up for the rest of the night, rubbing and scratching. Every morning, I have swollen eyes and a bleeding head. My aunt and uncle take me to a doctor. He says it'll take time for me to adjust. This continues for a year.

My aunt tries to fatten me up and pushes food into me. I see her mix my glass of milk with cream and put extra calories in everything she makes. I still can't eat too much at one time. I'm so thin that my aunt and uncle become very worried. They take me to Nantasket Beach for the summer to build me up.

They rent a couple of rooms across from the beach. I love it. This is the first time I've been in the ocean. It's cold, but it feels wonderful on my skin. My aunt puts lotion on me so I won't burn. I spend most of the day swimming. I meet kids who are playing some kind of game with a ball and a drawn square in the sand. They call it boxball and ask if I want to play. I've never played this game, but after watching them for a while I catch on. Then I join them and have a great time. We keep moving and don't talk much. The little English I know is enough for them to understand me.

I get up early every morning and play boxball with the boys. When we get tired we go in the water and fool around, throwing the ball and dunking each other. We play into the late afternoon until my Aunt Sadie comes to get me.

That summer, my appetite is much better. I'm not alone as much and I don't have so many nightmares.

My Aunt Vera and Uncle Max come to visit us from New York. She's my mother's other sister, the one who sent all the CARE packages to us in Europe and got me out of Ellis Island. She doesn't look as much like my mother as Aunt Sadie does, but she's very warm and keeps grabbing me to give me a big hug. I pretend I don't like it, but I do. She says I look just like my mother. She brings me presents and tells me to come visit her soon. She has grown sons and I'll be able to meet them. We take pictures and they put me in the middle in front.

I know my new family loves and cares for me, but I am always thinking about Uncle Yossef and my cousins and wonder if I'll ever see them again.

Wishing my father dead and leaving my mother to die is always on my mind. I feel guilty about surviving whenever I have a good time. I don't deserve to be happy.

CHAPTER 22:
SCHOOL AND REUNION

I CAN'T SPEAK English very well, and I have a bad stutter. The boys make fun of me and chase me to school every morning. They say, "Learn English, and we'll stop hitting you."

I listen to the Lone Ranger on the radio and practice my English by pronouncing the words I hear. I wish I could say those words without an accent.

The school puts me in the fourth grade. To help me catch up, my home room teacher sends me to spend some time in first, second and third grade every day. I am tutored by the smartest kid in each class. In first grade, a little kid teaches me the alphabet. In second grade a student helps me with pronunciation. In third grade, the smart student helps me improve my writing. In my fourth grade class, a girl reads to me. I learn English in four months, but I can't lose my accent. I beg my home room teacher for help.

She says, "Go home and sit in front of the mirror every day and stick out your tongue and say 'the', not 'de' or 'dze', but 'the'. Pronouncing 'th' correctly is the key to losing your accent. When you say it the right way, there will be steam condensation on the mirror."

I practice for weeks and finally see steam on the mirror. I master "the" and I lose my accent.

The boys stop beating me up. Now they only tease me because I stutter.

School is torture. The anxiety of being called on is unbearable. The nights before recitation are the worst. I know I'll be asked to sit down.

The teacher calls on me. After all the snickers and giggles she says, "You may sit." I wish I were dead.

My Uncle wants me to have a bar mitzvah and insists that I go to Hebrew school. I'm sick and tired of the kids laughing at me because I stutter. When I hear one of the Hebrew school boys making fun of me, I throw a brick into his stomach and knock him unconscious. The teacher yells and screams at me and I'm expelled from Hebrew school.

I don't have a bar mitzvah.

Uncle Yossef, and my cousins Leah, Uri, Ilya and Ruth come to America in 1949. It's good to hear Uncle Yossef's voice after all this time. He says that he and the cousins want to see me and my aunt and uncle. They settle in New York where Aunt Vera rents two apartments for them. One for Ilya and Ruth and the other for Uncle Yossef, Leah and Uri. They all will work for Uncle Max and adjust to life in America.

The three of us drive to New York and stay in Aunt Vera's house. It is a big, beautiful house. Aunt Vera is busy cooking and baking for our reunion. When we arrive everyone has gathered to greet us. Aunt Vera says, "Chiel, you're getting so handsome." She pulls me into her arms and gives me a big squeeze. I feel my cheeks getting warm and pretend I don't like her display of affection. But I really do.

We're all talking at once and so happy to see each other. Ruth tells me how tall I am now and musses my hair. Ilya gives me a bear hug and Leah kisses my face all over. I get a little punch from Uri and both he and Uncle Yossef hug me at the same time.

Ruth and Ilya are expecting a baby, and Leah invited her boyfriend, Ben. They tell us they plan to get married soon.

At the dinner table, Uncle Yossef says, "Thank you, God, for blessing us and for our being together again." He says another prayer for family no longer with us.

After dinner we reminisce about the funny things we experienced during the war and the sad things as well.

We drive back to Boston early Sunday morning after making a date to get together in Boston soon. I think about the weekend. How wonderful to see my family, but I'm sad to be leaving them once more. I guess it's something I need to get used to. I've learned to love my Aunt Sadie and Uncle Josh. They've given me a home. But they're very cold. Neither of them can show affection for me. My uncle is extremely nervous and paranoid. He can't forget his experience in the concentration camp. The atmosphere in our house is doom and gloom

This trip reminded me of the easy warmth of Uncle Yossef's family. I'm glad Ilya and Ruth are so happy and looking forward to their baby and Leah will be married soon. Maybe someday I'll have a family of my own too.

Full of love and happiness. With no fear, only love and trust.

CHAPTER 23:
ADOPTION

THE SOCIAL WORKER has been coming to our house over the years. When I'm fourteen, she decides I can be adopted.

Aunt Sadie says, "Chiel, now you should choose an American name and take our last name.

What do you think about Charles? It starts with the same letters and we can call you Charlie." "I hate that name, Aunt Sadie. I'd rather be called Philip."

"Okay, your name will be changed from Chiel Salpeter to Philip Jochnowitz."

Uncle Josh says, "Now that you're our legal son, how do you feel about calling us Mom and Pa?"

"That's good."

I don't mind calling him Pa, and I'm glad he doesn't want me to call my aunt, 'Mama.' That's what I called my mother, Shanna. Again I think about my mother and know she'd be happy that I'll be part of a regular family. Pa pats me on the back and Mom gives me a brief hug.

Except for oral recitations I do very well in school. In the eighth grade, I take the entrance exam for Boston Latin, a very prestigious school. Not everyone has an opportunity to attend. I pass the test and am admitted the following year. Boston Latin assigns a tremendous amount of home work. I study very hard and it pays off. I receive the Certificate of Approbation with Distinction: the highest honor. Pa carries the certificate in his wallet. He shows it to everybody. I'm glad he's so proud of me.

Boston Latin gets harder. I don't want to do all that studying, so I quit. When I tell Mom, she's mortified, "Philip, you gave up a wonderful opportunity."

"I know, Mom. Right after I quit I was sorry. Do you think you can help me get back in?"

She calls the principal and asks him to take me back. He says, "No, there are others who are anxious to attend. We don't want anyone who doesn't appreciate this chance."

The following year I go to Roxbury High School. The kids there are tough and expect me to be tough. I change the way I comb my hair and wear different clothes so I look like the other gang members. I hang out in a pool room. One night coming home after playing pool, some kids follow me. I start running but they catch up. The leader yells, "You think you're tough, huh?" He jumps me and beats me up with brass knuckles.

The next morning my face is a mess, so I start carrying a knife when I'm out after dark. When my parents see the knife, they decide to move to a safer community.

We move to Brookline, Massachusetts where the kids

aren't part of gangs, the neighborhood is quieter and life is better. I borrow my father's car almost every Friday night, pick up my friends, go out for Chinese food and a movie. I like these guys better than the gang in Roxbury.

I go to court to become a U.S. citizen. Because I appear with my DA haircut, long sideburns, a blue suede jacket and blue suede shoes, the judge asks, "Are you looking for "juvenile court?"

I ace the exam and walk out of the courthouse. I know I look silly as I wave my little flag, but I don't care. I'm very proud to be an American.

After graduating from Brookline High school in 1955, I attend Boston University and major in English Literature. I like college, but don't do much homework and cram for tests to get good marks. I don't speak any better and keep to myself taking out my frustrations by careless driving. My father is annoyed with my frequent fender benders. "What's wrong with you, Philip?"

I feel bad that I upset my father. He's been pretty good to me and doesn't deserve this aggravation. "You're right, Pa. I don't know why I do these things. I'm sorry."

To blow off steam I begin lifting weights. I start to look great and the girls flirt with me. They think I'm the strong silent type, because I don't talk much. I date a couple of them, but we have nothing in common.

I become angrier each year and can't express it because there's no one to listen. My parents pay for me to see a psychiatrist. She has thick glasses and speaks softly. I like her because when I tell her about my childhood and guilt feelings she cries. She puts out a box of tissues for me, but she uses most of them. I talk and scream at her for three years, and she helps me understand and deal with my anger. Thanks to her, I feel better about myself.

On weekends I work for my father-washing windows and floors to help pay for tuition at Boston University. Sometimes I do a floor washing by myself, but when it's a big job, we work together. I'm beginning to understand and appreciate my father.

One night we're washing floors at the offices of one of his customers, and Pa's as fussy as ever. "Philip, don't forget to do the corners."

I hear a loud crash and see my father sprawled on the floor. He's holding his chest. "Something is wrong, Philip." He whispers.

I don't like his color or his short breaths so I call 911. After I take my sweater off, roll it up and put it under his head, I see he's breathing a little bit easier.

"Take it easy, Pa. They'll be here soon." Please God, don't let him die.

When the ambulance arrives the attendants think it's a heart attack and put an oxygen mask on his nose. Pa gives me a thumbs-up. He knows how worried I am.

When we get to the hospital, the doctor confirms my father suffered a heart attack. I call my Mom and tell her I'll pick her up. She cries all the way to the hospital. I'm fighting tears too.

After the doctor examines him thoroughly, he says, "He'll be all right, but he must take it easy." Pa's color is back and he smiles at me. "I guess I scared you, huh?"

I say a silent prayer of thanks.

His recovery is uneventful. I take over his business for a whole summer while he gets better.

I join the National Guard Reserves even though I'll need to go into the active Army after I graduate.

I say to my mother, "Have you noticed how much weaker Pa is? You're always talking about retiring in Israel. Now is the time to do it."

"No, Philip, I don't want to leave you."

"Mom, after I serve in the Army for six months, I want to be on my own, anyway." "But you'll be alone."

"I'm serious, Mom. Pa shouldn't be working so hard."

"Maybe you're right. This might be the right time to make the move."

I'm sad. I won't see them for a long time. But this is best for my parents. They're good people and they deserve to enjoy the rest of their lives.

CHAPTER 24:
THANK YOU

I'M SITTING IN the reception area of a Boston engineering firm and waiting to be interviewed. Just last
week, I was discharged from the Army. My good friend
Mark and I found an apartment in Brookline, Massachusetts. With my parents in Israel, I needed a place to live.
We signed the lease but now my funds are in deep trouble.

This opening is for a blueprint clerk. A low level job,
not what I really want to do, but I need the money *fast*.
It will keep me fed while I search for a writing position.
There probably won't be many applicants who have as
much education, so my hopes are high.

A young woman walks in the room. She has short, curly hair, pretty eyes and a nice smile. She's wearing a dark suit and colorful blouse. "Hi Philip. My name is Blanche Rubin. I'm the office manager." She shakes my hand and I follow her to an office. After we're seated she gets my pertinent information. She has a strong Boston accent and a nice smile. I really could get used to seeing her every day. She asks, "Why do you want this job?"

Should I make something up about how I always wanted to be a clerk? Of course not. I tell her the truth. "I need the money, am dependable and have excellent references, and if you hire me, I expect to work here for a reasonable length of time."

She flashes a smile. "I appreciate your honesty. I'll let you know after your references are checked."

The next day I find out the job is mine and start work the following week. My desk is in a large blueprint room where there are many young engineering co-op students behind drafting tables. Blanche uses the copier near my desk and chats with me while copies are running. Our talks are becoming more frequent and we've become comfortable with each other. I've grown to like her a lot and want to ask her out, but don't have the guts.

After a year, I land a good editing job. When I give Blanche the required two week notice, I muster up courage and grab my last chance.

"I'm inviting most of the people in the office to a going away party I'm giving for myself Would you be interested in acting as my hostess?"

What a way to get a date. I'm not so sure she'd go on a real date with me but I'm pretty sure she'll help me so I play it safe. I was right. She says, "I'll be glad to help."

The party was the start of a serious relationship and after several months, we decide to get married.

Once we're officially engaged, I call my Uncle Yossef and cousins. When I tell them about my fiance, they insist on meeting her. I don't want to take any time off from my new job, so we fly to New York one Saturday morning, and I introduce Blanche to my family. We gather at Leah's house where we have an early dinner. They all love her and are excited that I found someone who will make me happy at last. We fly back the same night so we can rest the following day and return to work on Monday.

Today is June 23, 1962, our wedding day. Blanche and I meet the family at the airport, take them to a hotel and spend some time with them. Then I drive her home to prepare for tonight. I'm at my apartment with Mark, my best man.

My mind is swirling. I think back to the beginning of my life's journey and all that has happened. How I resented what life offered me and almost lost my faith. My uncle's wise words come back to me. "I promise some day you'll be free and happy."

Even though Modeh Ani *(I give thanks)* is traditionally said in the morning, I feel it's appropriate to say it now. My long nightmare is over and my life and faith are restored. Before the happiest time of my life, I bow my head:

Modeh Ani

I offer thanks before you, living and eternal King, for You have mercifully restored my soul within me. Your faithfulness is great. Amen

B F JOCHNOWITZ, born and educated in Boston, Massachusetts, has always been passionate about writing. She and her husband owned and operated a publishing firm in Marblehead, Massachusetts—specializing in editing and typesetting college textbooks. After moving to Florida, she wrote this first book—a tribute to the life of her husband.

She is now writing a series of mystery novels which will be published in the near future.